FURTHER LIGHTS

FURTHER LIGHTS:

The Veda and the Tantra

T. V. Kapali Sastry

GYAN

Published by

Gyan Publishing House
5, Ansari Road
Daryaganj, New Delhi-110002
Phone: 011-47034999, 9811692060
E-mail: books@gyanbooks.com

Distribution Network
gyanbooks.com
India, USA, Canada, UK, Australia

ISBN: 978-93-6280-289-7 (HB)
First Published, 1951

2nd Impression 2024

Printed at: Gyan Press, Delhi.

FURTHER LIGHTS
Author: T. V. KAPALI SASTRY

FURTHER LIGHTS:

The Veda and the Tantra

T. V. KAPALI SASTRY

PREFACE

There have been two lines of higher thought occult and ultra-mundane that have governed the religious and spiritual mind of India ancient and mediaeval, and to a considerable extent the devout Hindu of modern times. The Veda and the Tantra, known as Agama, are the scriptural authority and support for the earnest faith in the revealed nature of these sacred texts. Among certain sections of the learned classes, the Tantra is supposed to contradict the Veda. A perusal of the Second Section of this book will remove the misconception. Even so, among a large section of the learned classes, the Veda in the main is only meant for rituals, *karma*, and real spiritual knowledge is to be found only in the Upanishads. This notion also will be uprooted on a close reading of the First Section.

It is to be noted that occult truths are there in the Veda while its main object is spiritual. It is also true that the spiritual aim is admitted as the goal in the Tantra while deliberating on the occult side of the teachings. These two scriptures, the Veda and the Tantra, which form the authority for the modern religious mind have been taken up for illustration in this book.

The First Section, based upon my Sanskrit Commentary on the Rig Veda, contains three articles, the first of which is in substance a reproduction in English of the 4th part of the Introduction, *Bhumika*, while the second is a discourse on the workings of the Mystic Fire, *Agni*, and the higher Powers he brings down to fill the being of the awakened soul engaged in the Vedic Yoga; to expound this idea is given a clear exposition of the 13th Hymn in the First Mandala of the Rig Veda commented upon in the *Siddhāñjana*; the third which exemplifies the fact that the Vedic rituals are symbolic of occult and spiritual Knowledge is based on the same commentary on the 28th Hymn of the First Mandala.

These studies were originally published in the Annuals that are devoted to Sri Aurobindo's teachings. Except the first and the last in the Second Section, which appeared in the Annual Numbers 6 & 7 of the Sri Aurobindo Circle, Bombay, the rest were all contributed to the Annual Numbers 6, 7, 9 and 10 of the Sri Aurobindo Pathamandir, Calcutta.

T. V. KAPALI SASTRY

CONTENTS

Section One

SECTION ONE

GODHEAD AND THE GODS IN THE RIG VEDA

WE propose to consider the question of the Vedic Gods with special reference to Agni in this brief study. If symbolism is the key for the interpretation of the hymns of the Rig Veda in the inner sense as expounded by Sri Aurobindo, then by implication it applies to the discovery of the true character of the Vedic Gods some of whom are identified with the powers of Nature in the physical world, as Sun, Moon, Heaven, Earth, Fire, Wind, Waters and the others who are according to modern scholars personified natural forces at work in the Universe. There is no doubt that in the early ages people worshipped Nature-Gods in many countries, as in India, Greece or Rome. But it is not correct to say that the people of the Vedic times deified or personified the forces of Nature; rather they believed that there were Gods who presided over the

Sun and the Moon, the Earth or Heaven, the Fire, the Storm, the sacred Rivers and other visible bodies in the physical universe. When they speak of Surya the Sun-God they have in mind for their object of worship the Deva who presides over the Solar body; the same is true with the other Gods in the Veda in so far as they are identified beyond doubt with the workings of the natural forces in the world. But the Gods of the Veda were much more than the physical description given of them whether in the hymns or by the scholars. If the Sun and Storm and Wind and Waters and other objects of Nature were all that sum up the Gods of the Vedic pantheon, albeit with their presiding Deities, then the modern theory about the primitive Vedic people would be perfectly plausible. These ancients, then, had not emerged from the primitive barbarism, were still governed by the crude religious beliefs in the efficacy of sacrifice to their Gods. They believed that their prayers were effective means to bring them all material blessings, rains from heaven, to release the waters from the clouds and help loosen the grip of Night on the Sun. But the true character of the Gods as it emerges from the hymns themselves does not agree with this account hazarded by modern scholarship for which the Brahminical ritualism elucidated by Sayana is to some extent responsible. For the gross and physical aspect of the Vedic worship though applicable in certain hymns does not apply in many, does not at all hold good throughout, but fades away as we proceed from hymn to hymn of sage after sage in all the ten Books of the Samhita. There are whole hymns which in the exoteric sense do not make sense at all. The ritualistic meaning can not be maintained throughout. And in order to achieve the impossible, impossible constructions are invented and with laborious effort we arrive at a result which leaves us wondering at the grotesque mentality of the Vedic bards; or in such places the meanings of the hymns are empty of any worthy idea or presentation of truth, a thought-content commensurate with the repute of Knowledge associated with the Veda. The Herculean effort made to dive deep into the water bears fruit in discovering the potsherd. The necessity of the symbolic interpretation arises from the unsatisfactory results of the labours of modern scholarship with the help of Sayana's ritualistic commentary. For apart from the poverty of thought and incoherence in the language of the sages assumed without warrant for the purpose of arriving at some sort of a cogent idea conveyed by the hymns, the learning does not take into account the ages-old tradition that the Vedas are the original source of spiritual Wisdom and Divine Knowledge.

When we seize the clues afforded by the deliberate symbolism devised by the Vedic seers in the hymns, we get admitted into the secrets of the Vedic Godhead, to the true character of the Gods, as seen and understood by the Rishis of the Rig Veda. Let us then seek for the truth in the original texts themselves and hear what the Rishis speak of the Gods and leave aside for the time being what others say about the Rishis or the Gods or what the moderns think the Gods must have been to the primitive poets of the Vedic age. A presentation of the Gods in general with their special and general function and nature as described in the Riks will facilitate our enquiry into Agni, the Deity who is usually first hymned by most sages of the Rig Veda.

The question then arises: who are these Gods, Agni, Indra, Surya, Varuna, Mitra, Ashwins and a host of others addressed in the hymns? Moderns tell us that the Aryans of the Vedic times had susceptible minds, were easily impressionable, thought and believed all natural forces and phenomena to be bristling with life and intelligence and endowed with power to bestow benefits on them in return for the sacrifice and so they offered their prayers to them. What are these natural objects and forces that appeared to these early semi-civilised peoples as figuring and embodying the Gods? They are the blue expanse above, *dyauh*, the earth with her luxuriant vegetation and green meadows below, *prithivi*, the sun, source of all light and life, *surya*, the lovely dawn, *ushas*, the flowing rivers, *nadyah*, and the cool life-giving waters, *apah*, Maruts, the storms that rush through the sky, Indra who with his thunderbolt, *vajra*, deals a death-blow to the clouds and sends down rain. Modern learning avers further that in its childhood the Aryan humanity was possessed of a hankering after light and turned away from darkness and naturally could not suppress its wonder at the sight of fire when it was produced by the friction of the churning sticks, *arani*! Hence next to Indra, Agni is the most important God in the Vedic pantheon.

This account of the Gods is based largely on conjectures and the assumptions that there could not have been real spirituality or sublime conception of the Godhead in those primitive times. The Gods as they reveal themselves in the hymns do not throughout answer to this description, though the Riks in many places torn from the context may lend support to this view because of the external and physical aspect that is generally maintained for the purposes of outer worship and ceremonial rite. But there are many hymns scattered over all the Mandalas of the

Rig Veda which not only do not testify to the correctness of this picture but contradict the external sense, overshadow the physical aspect and proclaim the spiritual and psychological functions of the Gods and their Cosmic character. There are a number of instances out of which we shall take up a few to show that the Riks cease to give us any meaning that is applicable to the physical aspect, to the Nature-gods of the naturalistic and ritualistic interpreters. When the Rik says[1] "The wise always see the highest step, the supreme abode of Vishnu like an eye extended in heaven",[2] assuming that *paramam padam* is not the supreme abode but the highest step which is the meridian and that Vishnu is the sun, how can the wise see him *always*, *sadā*? If it is the sun in the physical universe that is seen, then it cannot be seen always in the

[1] In this study all the references are to the Rig Veda unless specially indicated. The English renderings keep close to Sri Aurobindo's line, but his own translations, where available, are given marked with asterisks.

[2] 1.22.20 तद् विष्णोः परमं पदं सदा पश्यन्ति सूरयः। दिवीव चक्षुराततम्॥

meridian. Nor can it be said that the wise alone see him always in the meridian who is not so visible to others who are not wise. It will then be either absurd and fanciful or it must be the invisible Sun, not the physical one, who is always visible in his Supreme Abode to the eye of the Wise. Let us take another instance where the seer Praskanva says, "Beholding the loftier light that springs up above the Darkness we have come to the Sun, the God among Gods, the most excellent (loftiest) light."[1] Here does it make sense if the light loftiest is taken to mean the physcial sun of our system? It does not, and that is why a European scholar suggests that this is an allusion to a spiritual Sun and darkness here means sin, as Sayana suggests as an alternative. "The approach to the Sun intimates the reunion with the supreme spirit. We attain to the best light, *aganma jyotir uttamam*." Or let us take the instance of Indra, the most important of the Vedic

[1] 1.50.10 उद्वयं तमसस्परि ज्योतिष्पश्यन्त उत्तरम् ।
देवं देवत्रा सूर्यमगन्म ज्योतिरुत्तमम् ॥

Gods according to scholars. This most powerful king of Gods, the warrior with his thunderbolt dealing death-blow to the clouds giving us rain is generally recognised beyond doubt to be a deity ruling somewhere far above the region of the clouds. But when we study the hymns addressed to him—leaving aside those in which the veil of symbols is either too thick or too thin—those which can be plainly construed, we are confronted with passages that betray the shallowness of the contention that Indra represents like other Gods of the Veda nothing but a phenomenon of Nature. Let us take at random a couple of instances that throw light on the spiritual and really Divine and not physical and fanciful character of Indra. "Far is that Name secret, by which the worlds called to thee",[1] or "Great is that secret Name longed for by many by which thou madest what was and what shall be",[2] or, again, when the Rishi Babhru says, "His strong and secret

[1] X. 55.1 दूरे तन्नाम गुह्यं ...यत् त्वा ...अह्वयेताम् ...

[2] X. 55.2 महत्तन्नाम गुह्यं पुरुस्पृग्येन भूतं जनयो येन भव्यम्।

abode I have seen; desiring him who founds, I got at (his abode). I asked of others, they said, 'being men of leading, awakened, let us attain to Indra.'"[1] Here again what is the secret place, is it a little or far above the region of the clouds? Does not the Rishi plainly state that the very fact of awakening, *bubudhana*, leads to Indra, once there is the longing and that the founder, *nidhāta*, cannot be a fanciful being somewhere in the middle or the higher regions of the sky? Is the awakening simply waking up from sleep? Maruts or storm-gods more than the other Vedic Gods have a pronouncedly physical character in their functionings in most of the hymns addressed to them. Even here it is difficult to ignore their psychological and spiritual function that is the real and inner aspect. Now Agastya calls upon the Maruts praying for their protection so that the man they loved may be saved not only from ruin

[1] V. 30.2 अवाचचक्षं पदमस्य सस्वरुग्रं निधातुरन्वायमिच्छन् ।
अपृच्छमन्यां उत ते म आहुरिन्द्रं नरो बुबुधाना अशेम ॥

but from sin also, *aghāt rakshata.*[1] By appeasing the Wind and the storm-gods the houses and property of the man who is their favourite may not become the target of their fury and thus he may be said to be saved from ruin. But how can he be saved from *sin*? Vasishtha sings, "Here, here, ye of self-grown strength, seers with skin of Sun's splendour, O Maruts, I dedicate to you this sacrifice."[2] Note that the Wind and the Storm-god is evanescent here, takes on the resplendent garb of solar colour and assumes seer-hood also. It is no wonder that the same seer sings, "He is a sage, the illumined thinker, Dhira, who knows these mysteries what the mighty *Prishni* bore in her udder."[3] These secrets are and can be known only by the enlightened sage and not the common man, asserts Vasishtha. Among the Vedic Gods no God is better known and identified whose func-

[1] I. 166.8

[2] VII. 59.11 इहेह वः स्वतवसः कवयः सूर्यत्वचः। यज्ञं मरुत आवृणे ॥

[3] VII. 56.4 एतानि धीरो निण्या चिकेत पृश्निर्यदूधो मही जभार ॥

tion is unmistakable and never-failing than Soma. But the many things that are spoken of Soma cannot at all apply to the creeper, the material object which is purely a symbol in the outer sacrifice. There is no help if one is carried away by flights of fancy and assumes with an extraordinary unreasoning that the Vedic sages got too much drunk to distinguish the inanimate from the animate, the insentient from the sentient and in their intoxication fancied the presence of a deity in the draught of Soma. Here we may note in passing that the Soma plant is an extinct species and it was not easily available even thirty centuries ago. Twenty-four varieties of Soma plant are mentioned along with the places of their growth and their therapeutic virtues, such as strength and longevity in the Sushruta Samhita (Chikitsa-sthana, Chap. 29), but the intoxicating property is not mentioned. It is difficult to imagine how sage after sage in hymn after hymn goes on singing the glory of this intoxicating drug. Surely there must be a measure even for depraved addicts. But still the hymns, though on the surface, may refer to the plant for ceremonial worship, consistently drive at the psychological, occult and spiritual side of the truth. And some Riks cannot be properly construed at all if the Soma is taken to mean the drug. What are we to say when the Veda plainly hymns, "O Thou, all-seeing, the illumining rays of thee, who art the lord, encompass all the abodes; Soma, with thy natural powers thou pervadest (the all) and flowest, thou art the king and lord of the whole world"?[1] Another Rik openly decides the question of Soma. "When they crush the herb, one thinks that he has drunk the Soma; but no one ever tastes him whom the Brahmans know to be the Soma."[2]

Usha is rightly identified with Dawn, but even here her attribute cannot apply always to the physical sunrise. Does she speak sweet and true words, *sunrita*—a term which is repeatedly applied to her? Kakshivan addresses her: "Following the course of the Ray of Truth,

[1] IX. 86.5 विश्वा धामानि विश्वचक्ष ऋभ्वसः...पतिर्विश्वस्य भुवनस्य राजसि।

[2] X. 85.3 सोमं मन्यते पपिवान्....न तस्याश्नाति कश्चन॥

ritasya rashmim, bestow on us happy, happy knowledge-will".[1] Here Sayana admits that *rita* means Truth which is Sun in the context and the gross interpretation, of course, demands the extension of the meanings of words like *rita* to water, sacrifice, food and many others and this unreason is needed again for such numerous contexts indeed.

There are Mitra and Varuna, the Ashwins, other gods and goddesses whose identities are variously surmised and whose physical aspects are less pronounced than those we have referred to and for that reason we need not take up any of them here, as the Riks addressed will bear plain testimony to the psychological and inner significance, and to the Cosmic and spiritual functionings under different names and personalities of the Godhead. It is enough if we remember that the Gods whose identities with the objects and forces of Nature in the physical universe are quite assured are not really and deeply the external

[1] I. 123.13 ऋतस्य रश्मिं अनुयच्छमाना भद्रं भद्रं क्रतुमस्मासु धेहि ।

things meant as objects of ritual worship, but are much more and are intensely divine in their true form and nature, superb and intimate in their workings as powers of the Godhead in the hidden and occult layers of our being as well as in the Cosmic existence.

II

Now let us see if it is at all a fact that the hymns themselves speak of the Gods with different names and powers of the One supreme Godhead. The oft-quoted Rik of Dirghatamas is too well-known and there are a few others that have the same import that the One is named variously by the sages. And this fact is certainly important, but that is not enough to show the relation of the Gods among themselves or their position individually in relation to the One who is adored through each and all of them. For we can take them as mere names of the One, themselves without substance and form, distinct from one another or from the supreme One whose functions they represent. We shall present here in a general way the fact as emerging from the Riks themselves that the Gods of the Veda are not mere names but are different Powers, have different functions, distinctive signs that mark them out featuring their Personalities, yet not absolutely separate from but closely allied to one another, not apart from the sole Supreme Truth, the Godhead but definite manifestations of That indefinable.

It is advisable to convince ourselves that this our reading of the nature of the Vedic Gods is not an invention of our own but a discovery of the truth which was faintly seen and stated in unmistakable terms by Yaska who was after the Vedic age the first to probe into the secrets of the Gods, and openly acknowledged the impossibility of ordinary minds without *tapas*, spiritual force, understanding the nature of the Devatas. And we must remember in this connection that he was an etymologist and his interpretations are normally naturalistic. Though he admits the existence of other schools of Vedic interpreters and does not plainly condemn ritualism as such, still occasionally scouts the explanations given by the Brahmanas, the Vedic scripture for Ritualism. 'The Brahmanas speak liberally of many qualities'; often they are extravagant and fanciful in reading into the hymnal texts or into the Vedic Gods many imagined meanings or qualities. According to his commentator, Yaska hesitates to follow the Brahmanas in their explanations as they speak of everything in all possible ways and we ought not to swallow them, but the truth must be sought for.[1] Yaska gives us an information which is valuable for our purpose, coming as it does from one whose school of thought generally gives naturalistic meanings to the Vedic hymns while admitting the Supreme Soul, *Mahan Atma* as the God of Gods or the Sun as the Soul of all things mobile and immobile. In explaining the word *nir-riti* in two different senses, namely, earth and sin or suffering (*papma*, *duhkha*) he quotes a Rik from the

[1] निरुक्तम् VII. 24. "बहुभक्तिवादीनि ब्राह्मणानि" भक्तिर्नाम गुणकल्पना, येन केन चिद् गुणेन ब्राह्मणं सर्वं सर्वथा ब्रवीति, तत्र तत्वमन्वेष्यमेव भवति।

enigmatic hymns of Dirghatamas. He explains the few important words of the verse as he usually does and says that *nir-riti* is earth, construing the Rik in the naturalistic sense, at the same time points out that the wandering recluses, *parivrajakas*, say that it is suffering, *krichchram.* He says that in different contexts or in different schools the same word has different meanings and even then it is difficult to decide the import of certain Riks. Frequently there are possible doubts. Shakapuni, says Yaska, made up his mind to have knowledge of all the Deities. The Deity appeared before him with a double sign (Male and Female). He could not understand what it was and asked to be enlightened, saying, 'let me know thee.' The Deity directed him to a Rik (I.164.29) and said, "The Deity spoken of in this verse is myself." Now let us consider the import of this account of Yaska. A few facts are clear: to pin one's faith on the etymology of words alone as did the Nairuktas like Shakapuni could not give knowledge of the Gods; the Rik that the Deity mentioned must obviously refer to the One which holds in itself all the Gods or which is the substantial and the sole Deity of which all the Gods are various manifestations with their functions and names appropriate to them. Above all what is most astounding and almost incredible is the fact that the naturalistic interpretation of the Rik is persisted in by commentators, though Sayana refers lightly to the spiritual, *adhyatmic*, import of the Rik. The verse itself is plainly symbolic, rather enigmatic on the face of it, as are always the hymns of Dirghatamas and we need not enter into a discussion of its meaning as it involves an enquiry into many possible alternatives even though we may keep in mind the context of Shakapuni's episode mentioned by Yaska. Though not a ritualist, Yaska decidedly interprets the Gods of the Veda as those presiding over the forces of Nature and hence the leaning to the naturalistic interpretation is pronounced in his explanations. But he emphatically affirms that the Gods are not insentients, but conscious beings with cosmic functionings though they pertain more to the outer existence, i.e., to the physical universe. This is evident from the threefold classification of the Gods and their abodes as well as from the explanation he gives of the hymns which are addressed to inanimate objects in the Veda.

A common dwelling and common enjoyment entitle the objects and beings of a world to be treated as belonging to and part of that world, *samsthana-ekatwam*, *sambhoga-ekatwam*. His account of the Vedic Gods and the world-existence may be summed up in a few passages; that will help us to get an idea of the system of thought pertaining to the deities of the Vedic pantheon that prevailed among a section of Vedic interpreters who were not ritualists; but they assumed to depend for their conclusions on the Vedas, the hymns themselves and not on the Brahmanas or Upanishads though the latter seem to have been known to them as could be seen from certain sections, at least the supplement, *parishishta* of Yaska's Nirukta. Yaska's commentator Durgacharya explains the passages of Yaska on the Devatas with their character, abodes and functions in the light of Upanishadic thought.

Even though his explanations are quite plausible, we must avoid the suspicion that he read his own thought trained in the Upanishadic lore into the lines of the Nirukta. But Yaska himself gives in one or two short paragraphs what he understood to be the nature, work and place of the Vedic Gods as gathered from the hymns themselves and come down to him through the Nairukta tradition. There are three worlds, Earth, Middle region and the Sky which are the abodes of Agni, Vayu or Indra and Aditya respectively and above them all is the Mahan Atma; all the Gods, whatever their number, have their dwellings with one or other of these three Gods. They are born one of the other, the *prakriti* or nature of each is so flexible as to be modified into the nature of other Gods, *itaretara-prakritayah;* they are born as the fruit of works, *karma-janmanah.* Because of the magnificent opulence of the Deity, *mahabhagva,* the One Self *Eka Atma,* is lauded in many ways or as many. Of the One Atman other Gods are limbs; they are all born of the Atman; the Atman is their chariot, Atman is their horses, Atman is the weapon, Atman is the arrows, in short, Atman is the everything of the Gods (Nirukta VII.4). If all the Gods of all the worlds, their horses and chariots and weapons are all the One Devata, the One Atman, a misunderstanding may arise, viz., that really there is no difference among the Gods or between them and their vehicles etc. And to remove this possible misconception Yaska adds, because of the majestic power the Gods are endowed with, each Deity has different names and divides itself into different functionings and is accordingly hymned. That the various Vedic Gods have their many functions and names and that they are different Powers is admitted on all hands and there is no doubt or controversy on this point. As for their abodes it is a question that deserves to be considered at some length and that we shall do in determining the true character of the Gods.

Is the idea of the supreme Deity, the sublime Reality, as a fact of spiritual experience indicated, clearly expressed, in the hymns themselves generally or is it only a later bold conjecture or a vague idea ventured in a few later hymns and that it is only in the Upanishads the thought is developed as affirmed by modern scholars? This is the one question on which there have been conflicting views. We shall dispose of this first, for on this point hinges the whole question of the spiritual and true greatness of the Rishis of the Rig Veda. We shall take up a number of pertinent passages from many Mandalas of the Rik Samhita to show that That One, *tad ekam*, was known to the Rishis and it is That towards which they wend their way in the inner and secret path of the Sacrifice, with the help of the higher Powers, called Devas, limbs as it were, of the supreme Godhead functioning in the field of Cosmic action. We shall choose such texts as can be plainly construed and avoid passages which may require the elucidation of symbolic imagery in which the meanings of many hymns are clothed. First there stands the famous Rik of Dirghatamas: "Indra, Mitra, Varuna, Agni, they call him; and he is also the Heavenly Garutman of lovely plumage. The One Existent the illumined ones call variously, call it Agni, Yama, Matarishwa".[1]

In the third Mandala we have the idea of the One plainly mentioned as all that is and moves. "All beings that are born, they both (Earth and Heaven?) keep separate; bearing the great Gods, vexed they are not. The Universal One that rules over the immobile and the fixed (is) what walks, what flies, what is—this manifold birth."[2] This is an interesting verse and a fairly plain one and the construing of the sense offers no difficulty; and Sayana is helpful in giving the construction and the word-meaning but not the correct interpretation. Western scholars find the rudiments of the later Upanishadic thought here. It is interesting to note their views. Griffiths translating it quotes Wallis (*Cosmology of the Rig Veda*): We find mention in one hymn of a primordial substance or unit out of which the universe was developed. This is 'the one thing' (*ekam*) which we

[1] I. 164.46 इन्द्रं मित्रं...एकं सद्विप्रा बहुधा वदन्ति...आहुः।

[2] III. 54.8 विश्वेदेते जनिमा संविविक्तः महो देवान् ।बिभ्रती न व्यथेते...विश्वमेकं चरत् पतत्रि विषुणं विजातम्।

have met with in connection with the Aja the Unborn, (Book I, 164, 6, 46), and which is also used synonymously with the universe in accordance with the principle which is the key to much of the later mysticism that cause and effect are identical. The poet endeavours, in a strain which preludes the philosophy of the Upanishads, to picture to himself the first state of the world, and the first signs of life and growth in it." Again each of the twenty-two verses in the 55th Sukta of the third Mandala ends with the statement, "The powerful Might of the Gods is the Great One, *mahat devanam asuratwam ekam*". In Vamadeva's Hymns to Agni there is the expression *vapusham ekam*, which we find again in V. 62, 1. While the former is addressed to Agni, the latter to Surya—technically to *Mitra-Varunau*. Vamadeva sings: "Thou shining, black is thy path: thy light is in the front, thy moving splendour is the One of the embodied (gods)."[1]

[1] IV. 7.9 कृष्णं त एम रुशतः पुरोभाः चरिष्णु अर्चिर्वपुषामिदेकम्...

In the fifth Mandala: "There is a truth covered by a Truth where they unyoke the horses of the Sun: the ten hundreds stood together, there was that One (or That, the supreme Truth was one). I saw the greatest (best, most glorious) of the embodied gods."[1]

Or we can take a hymn from Bharadwaja: "An immortal Light set inward for seeing, a swiftest mind within in men that walk on the way. All the Gods with a single mind, a common Intuition, move aright in their divergent paths towards the One Will."[2] The seer's vision of the profound truth is expressed here with a transparent simplicity and a plain statement of all the Gods in their respective ways turned towards the One Will.

Vasishtha says,. "That one, Thy birth, was there when Agastya brought Thee here."[3]

[1] V. 62.1 ऋतेन ऋतमपिहितं ...तदेकं देवानां श्रेष्ठं वपुषामपश्यम् ।

[2] VI. 9.5 ध्रुवं ज्योतिर्निहितं दृशये...एकं क्रतुमभि वि यन्ति साधु ।

[3] VIII. 33.10 विद्युतो ज्योतिः...तत्ते जन्मोतैकं अगस्त्यो यत्त्वा...आजभार ।

In the last Book: "Where they regard the only One beyond the seven Rishis....";[1] or in the same hymn (in the sixth verse): "In the navel of the unborn the One was placed and there in that One all the worlds abide."[2]

Again in another place, "The One existent, beautiful of plumage, the illumined seers by their words formulate in many ways (or forms)."[3]

The few references we have given from many Books in the Rig Veda, not only from the last Book, are sufficient to show that the idea of That One, the Sublime Truth which is also the Deity of all deities is not a later development but is there throughout in the Vedic hymns though veiled or kept in the background in some places while in a few others it is plainly stated and quite overt. When we closely appreciate these facts and

[1] X. 82.2 ...यत्र सप्त ऋषीन् पर एकमाहुः।

[2] X. 82.6 ...अजस्य नाभावध्येकमर्पितं यस्मिन् विश्वानि भुवनानि तस्थुः।

[3] X. 114.5. सुपर्णं विप्राः कवयो वचोभिः एकं सन्तं बहुधा कल्पयन्ति।

study the hymns addressed to the Gods, Indra or Soma or even Maruts, not to speak of Agni and Surya we find these Gods derive their support and strength from That One and are themselves That One, and they, each in his own way, help man in his Heavenward travel of which the goal is the Supreme One. We can take for instance a few examples of Gods adored as and leading man to That One. In addressing the Maruts, Vasishtha says "Whose Name, resplendent, One alone, widely extended like a sea, for the joy of many like the enduring strength of ancestral heritage."[1]

In the Valakhilya Hymns we find a verse: "The One has become all this."[2]

The seer Nema in his communion with Indra says—verses 4 and 5 in the hymn of Nema are said to be the words of response from Indra—"O singer, look, here I by my greatness surpass all that is born, the followers

[1] VIII. 20.13 येषामर्णो न सप्रथो नाम त्वेषं शश्वतामेकमिद्भुजे । वयो न पित्र्यं सहः ॥

[2] VIII. 58.2 एकं वा इदं वि बभूव सर्वम् ।

of Truth increase me....the espousers of Truth ascend and approach me, as I, the One, am seated on the summit of Heaven."[1]

In another hymn, "The one son born of the three, the conquering, ruddy treasure, they send, the Immortals unassailed look over the happy places (planes) of the mortals."[2]

"Held by the seven thought-powers he pleases the unharming rivers who increase the One Eye."[3]

"The Might of the great Deva is the great One."[4]

"Here is one light for thee, there is another: enter close into the third Light. In the union of the body with the Light, grow beautiful, dear to the Gods in their supreme birthplace."[5]

[1] VIII. 100.4,5 अयमस्मि जरितः पश्य...ऋतस्य एकमासीनं हर्यतस्य पृष्ठे...।

[2] VIII. 101.6 ते हिन्विरे अरुणं जेन्यं वस्वेकं पुत्रं तिसृणाम्। ते धामान्यमृता मर्त्यानां अदब्धा अभिचक्षते ॥

[3] IX. 9.4 स सप्तधीतिभिर्हितः नद्यो अजिन्वदद्रुहः। या एकमक्षि वावृधुः।

[4] X. 55.4 महन्महत्या असुरत्वमेकम्।

[5] X. 56.1 इदं त एकं...प्रियो देवानां परमे जनित्रे।

III

These Gods are quite often spoken of as identical with the Supreme Godhead that has manifested out of its own substance and power and intelligence the many Gods for their functionings in the various spheres of his Cosmic existence. Therefore the Veda mentions Him as One who alone is the holder of the Names of all the Gods (X. 82. 3). But the Gods are distinct personalities with their respective activities; while each is important in his place and fulfils his purpose and is indispensable for the governing of the Cosmic order his individual importance or greatness must not be judged by the number of hymns addressed to them. "The importance of the Gods", says Sri Aurobindo, "has not to be measured by the number of hymns devoted to them or by the extent to which they are invoked in the thoughts of the Rishis, but by the functions which they perform. Agni and Indra to whom the majority of the Vedic hymns are addressed are not greater than Vishnu and Rudra, but the functions which they fulfil in the internal and external world were the most active, dominant, directly effective for the psychological discipline of the ancient mystics. This alone is the reason of their predominance." The Sun, the glorious symbol of the Truth, the supreme Godhead of the Veda, is referred to as That One, *tad ekam*, addressed in fewer hymns than Indra or Agni or even Maruts. The Rishis invoke the powers of Agni and Indra because they are of constant and immediate consequence in the psychological and spiritual discipline of these mystics, and hence the importance and not because they are superior to the Sun; similarly Maruts, children of Rudra are not greater than their Father though there are more hymns addressed to them than to Rudra in the Rig Veda. The same may be said of Vishnu and Rudra to whom lesser number of hymns are devoted and yet Indra and Agni are not greater than they.

All the gods have their Cosmic functions in the universe, and their workings as psychological and spiritual powers within man is the central thought with which we are concerned in our reading of the Veda in its esoteric sense. Whatever their province of influence and action be in the external universe, the benefit of their presence and activity is always open to man when he has grown enough to discover the means to enlarge his existence with and to enter into the region of their help and influence. And that means is the same instrumentation by which the supreme One, the Creative Godhead produced, manifested, or created the Universe of Many, the world of creatures out of his own being. It is the giving of Himself, something of His substance for the building of the worlds, their beings and their governing powers in the Cosmic existence. This giving is Sacrifice, *Yajna*, in the Vedic system. If the Supreme Purusha by self-giving made possible the creation of this world-existence with its countless variety of living beings of which the most grown-up is the human being, man also can by self-giving earn the help of the Gods, of the higher Powers of the Godhead to new-create himself in the Spirit. For

Sacrifice is the Law instituted by the creative Godhead, the Purusha for self-extension in the world-existence, it is the Law by which creation is sustained, and it is also the Law by which enlargement and growth into the image of the immortal Godhead is made possible. This secret of the true and inner sacrifice was a common knowledge of the Vedic mystics, while the external Yajna was maintained as a symbol for ceremonial worship for the people in general.

Mortal man, the sages knew, could renew his birth by an interchange with the higher Powers, the cosmic Gods, the Immortals, who are the sons of Aditi, the Mother Infinite. For the supreme Godhead is not only He, but also She, in the infinitude of his calm potency for boundless extension, for measuring out his measureless powers in the Cosmic embodiment. This Infinite in the Veda is sometimes imaged as the ocean, *samudra*. And there is an upper ocean whence the creation and creative powers proceed downwards and over the Earth, while there is an inner ocean, *antah samudra*, to which the mystic gains access by special discipline, in and through the heart. He thus begins to enter the inner existence and lives the inner life by deepening his existence within and offering his possessions and whatever he is to the Gods who rule over and really own him and his universe of thoughts, feelings and experiences, for their acceptance. They in their turn bestow on him something of themselves, their light, their strength, the riches of the Immortal world to which they belong. He progresses from the depths of his being upwards to the abode of the higher powers leading to the Home of Truth where reigns the Sublime Effulgence. But he does not effect his journey at a stretch and reach the destination, nor does he commence and proceed with this up-hill task by his own strength either. It is with the help, the light and strength of the Gods which he receives in return for his self-giving, he is urged to his upward march in the path of the sacrifice. This offering is so nourishing to the Gods that they are born in him and increase their own substance in him; they are called the twice-born, *dwijanmānah*, for they are first born in the

Cosmos as the higher Powers of the Godhead, and their second birth takes place in man as the fruit of the sacrifice, thereby displacing his mortality, giving him his rightly won lift towards the higher altitudes of his being, to the Home of the Immortals, towards the sole Supreme, That One, for whose attainment all sacrifice is made, all *tapasya* undertaken, and all life, the whole being, dedicated.

This upward procession, then, is not effected at a stretch, there are many stages, many steps, *padani*, many stations, *dhamani*, through which one has to ascend as one climbs up a hill passing from one plateau to another, *sanoh sanum āruhat*. The Veda speaks of seven steps or places or worlds, at times of four, *chatushpad*, or five orders of being, five births, *pancha janah*. But we meet with three worlds and steps quite commonly which, as is well known, is the triple world of Earth, *prithivi*, Middle-world, *antariksha*, and Heaven, *dyauh*. These three are located in the outer existence and are used to represent the first three levels of inner existence, though there are still higher ranges overtopping this threefold layer of being and reaching out to the vaster and more luminous regions of the Cosmic ladder at the summit of which is the Home of the Eternal Truth, the Immortal Light, the Ineffable Beatitude.

But this Godward journey is not a smooth running, not without vicissitudes; there are the sons of Darkness, forces of Evil, Rakshasas, Asuras, to hinder the progress, even as there are forces of Good, the sons of Light, the Gods, to help our onward march. "We have to call in the aid of the Gods to destroy the opposition of these powers of Darkness who conceal the Light from us or rob us of it....we have to invoke the Gods by the inner sacrifice ....the Gods are not simply poetical personifications or abstract ideas or psychological and physical functions of nature....they are living realities....the soul of man is a world full of beings, a kingdom in which armies clash to help or hinder a supreme conquest, a house where the Gods are our guests and which the Demons strive to possess....the vicissitudes of human soul represent a Cosmic struggle not merely of principles and tendencies but of the Cosmic Powers which support and embody them. These are the Gods and Demons on the world-stage and in the individual Soul the same real drama with the same personages is enacted." (Sri Aurobindo)

The inner sacrifice, the real Yajna, then, is the way to reach the goal; it is indeed spoken of as a journey or voyage; it ascends, travels, hence is called *adhwa-ra*, pilgrim-sacrifice. The principle of sacrifice always exists in the creation; it is a latent power like electricity; to elicit it, the operation of a suitable apparatus is needed as in an electrical machine. Or it is conceived as a rolled-up thread of power; once it is unrolled it extends, *tantu*; it extends from here to Heaven forming a bridge, *setu*, or ladder by which the sacrificer ascends to the worlds above, communicates with the Gods. We gather such images of the sacrifice from the Brahmanas which explain the symbolic rituals of the Vedic worship. But they are profoundly significant and apply more truly to the inner Yajna. When the sacrifice in the ritual sense is conceived as a machinery in which every part is in its place and properly adjusted to the others and related to the whole or when it is imaged as a chain in which all the links are properly present and none is allowed to miss or when the Yajna is conceived to be a Purusha, a person with all the features of a human body, their deep and inner meaning becomes transparent to the sacrificer. All the different descriptions and the imagery unfailingly aim at the secret of the sacrifice —that it is at first in man a latent energy and once it is awakened by proper means it takes him up as on a lift to the regions of the higher Consciousness and does all that is necessary for the fulfilment of the Gods' purpose in him. But the sacrifice must be perfect, all the parts of one's being have to be willingly offered to the higher Powers, all the elements of the inner sacrifice must be prepared and properly arranged for the offering, so that the Gods may come down and accept his offerings and himself for their own strength and birth and growth in him for the Immortal ascension.

Even as every link has its place in a chain and every limb in a body, even so every one of the Cosmic Gods who has his part in the sacrificial session has his sanctified place in the scheme. Every portion of the Godhead, offered as sacrifice for the Cosmic creation, is entitled to receive its share in the inner sacrifice offered by man and it is indispensable that the entire body of the creative Purusha must be satisfied for the perfect fruition of the great work. It will be evident from what has been stated that the one element common to all the Gods is this that they are all Powers of the same Godhead, Sons of the Infinite and are Immortals, companions in the sacrifice, friends who offer their help to the sacrificer. Because of these general features common to the Gods we find them so addressed in some hymns that on the surface one is prone to think that each of the Gods does not differ from the others since he is hymned by the Rishis using the same appellation as the great God or the most beneficent or the supreme God himself. But this is only one aspect of the truth and does not abrogate the distinctness in their personalities and functions. For their distinguishing signs are clearly mentioned and in their special functions their individualities are always discernible. This is applicable to a very great majority of hymns while there are a few where the Gods concerned may be of a doubtful character. Apart from the Knowledge one can gather from the meaning of a hymn that a particular God is addressed, there is a technique given to us by which the Gods are distinguished. The colours, vehicles, weapons and the physiognomies of the Gods are mentioned in some hymns and these are symbolical, intimately expressive of the truth and character of the Gods visible to the inner vision of the Rishis. Yaska's Nirukta mentions the vehicles of Indra, Agni and other Gods. "Indra has two green horses, Agni's ruddy, Aditya's tawny, Ashwins have two donkeys and Pushan goats; antelopes of Maruts, rosy rays of Ushas and Savitr's dusky horses along with the vehicle of Brihaspati called Vishwarupa are mentioned and Vayu's horses are called Niyuta."[1] Again we gather from a hymn of Manu Vaivaswata (VIII.29) that

[1] निरुक्त–निघण्टु: 1. 25. हरी इन्द्रस्य...नियुतो वायोः ।

"Soma is brown, a youth active with a golden ornament; Agni is a luminous sage among the Gods; Twashtr the artisan holds iron knife in his hand; Indra has his thunderbolt; Rudra a pointed weapon strong with his healing medicines; Pushan watches all the ways like a thief; Vishnu with his mighty strides makes the Gods joyous; the Ashwins set their feet along with Ushas." From such references also we can learn the distinction that attaches itself severally to the various Gods of the Vedic pantheon. Their activities proceed from their original home which is the realm of the sublime Truth, for they are but different powers of the Godhead. But their immediate help and therefore importance depends upon the need in the various steps and the progress of the journey. As their field of activity is Cosmic in character and ranges from the high heights of this created existence down to the Earth-level, their dominant positions vary with the various rungs; and though each step in the onward march of the sacrifice is taken with the immediate help of one Power or other, one facet of the Godhead, it is really aided by all the Gods, all the Powers of the Godhead backing the frontal Personality whose importance is directly and immediately realised in this advancement. It is this fact that is the basis for the Rishis hymning several Gods and each one of them separately on different occasions and seeing the greatest God in him who is face to face in this occult and spiritual transaction into which the sacrificer enters.

It is needless to say that these powers of the Godhead are realities to the Vedic Rishi. He sees them not as a mere form or symbol of an idea with an uncertain visionary eye of mind but as tangible and quite concrete in their own kind, receives their influence and is benefited by their favour; strengthened by their gift he comes into direct contact with them, achieves a settled relationship that continues to the end or leads to the final consummation. Numerous are the hymns in which the many-sided relation established between the Deva and the Rishis is revealed to us. At times the Deva is realised as the father, guardian and protector and often he is the help, guide and friend; significantly, the God who is the Father becomes the Son of man, and all these relations do not detract from the eternal and immortal rulership of the Deity as the King of the Universe while mortal man, the awakened Rishi emerging from the murky waters of lower life rises in adoration, bows and pays his homage to the supreme Lord of the world and his Powers. This kind of relationship that the Vedic Rishis maintained with the Godhead has continued to exert its influence on later generations and in spite of the gulf between the Vedic times and later ages the tradition has lived down to our own days that man can worship God in that relation which is best suited to his temperament and competence. Or, it is truer to state that God chooses for the soul the kind of relation in which the type of the soul could most naturally commune with him—as father or mother, king or companion or child beloved.

We have in general terms spoken of the Vedic Gods, their general character as cosmic Powers functioning in the universe as well as in the individual, all having a common abode at the summit of the Creation but extending themselves and their activities over the whole range of Cosmic existence which has many steps or stages or what we may call planes of being: at the same time, they, each in his own way, dominate one plane or other with varying stress for their special functions. For these planes or levels of being, or steps in the staircase of creation, represent the variously constituted world-existence governed by the cosmic principles of Matter, Life, Mind and other still subtler and higher principles of divine order which are seven in number according to the Vedic seers. We have not here taken up the question of the special characteristics of the several Gods, much less their place and functions in the various stages of the sacrifice. That is a vast subject involving the explanation of the symbols employed in the outer sacrifice and then, their corresponding significances in the inner Yajna; and at every important stage of the discussion relevant hymns and passages and the ritualistic texts (Brahmanas) have to be mentioned in support of and as internal evidence for the correctness of our interpretation of the symbols in regard to the inner secret of the sacrifice and the true character of the Gods. But what we have stated so far is sufficient to give a general idea of the Gods as great and distinct powers of the supreme Godhead who come down to man when he has increased in stature to abide by the Law of sacrifice for the creation of the Godhead in him, even as the Godhead by sacrifice built the world of which he is a part.

To illustrate this truth we shall consider and confine ourselves to Agni the first God, enquire into the special functions he is associated with and ponder over his general and special attributes we come across in the Vedic hymns. We shall in the light of the hymns themselves deal with the important appellations with which the God is addressed and where necessary unveil the symbols in accordance with Sri Aurobindo's way of approach to the Vedic study. We choose this God for our enquiry here because he is nearer to us than others, is easily accessible and awakened in us and his immediate importance entitles him to first place in our adoration.

IV

Who is Agni the Fire, the God who is first awakened and adored by the Rishis? Surely it is not the third element, the principle of heat and light that is adored as God though that may be his symbol and form for worship in the physical existence. Nor can it be the sacrificial fire though that was the consecrated symbol for ritualistic worship in ancient times. And that cannot be Agni the God without whom 'the Immortals are not happy'. For it is said that Agni is the intuitive Knowledge of sacrifice and in him all the Gods take joy. He is the face and mouth of the Gods because the offerings to him he conveys to the Gods and fronts them in their approach to man to partake in the offerings and sacrifice. He is their messenger, for through him first, man communicates with the higher Powers; he is also the leader, Nara, and priest, Hota, of the sacrifice; he guides it and calls upon the Gods to be present and accept the offerings. Of all the Gods he is the first to be born in man; to the Cosmic God this is the second birth as his first is in the Cosmos; he is the Will, *Kratu*, of the Divine in man and once he is awakened, i.e., produced by Father Heaven and Mother Earth,—the tinders, *arani*, that strike out the sacrificial fire in the symbolic rite—he rises and grows heavenward fed by the offerings of the sacrificer, the human soul. This is the Flame whose original home is the great Heaven, but who is born in man, Immortal in the mortal. He is fostered by the seven Sisters, is the child of the seven Mothers, the seven Rivers, the Waters, nourish and support him—these are figures of the energies of the seven Cosmic principles. He has seven tongues because he contains in himself the seven essentials of the planes of Cosmic existence so that when he accepts the offerings with the seven tongues they reach and satisfy the needs of the seven planes of being into which the soul is to be born or which are to manifest in the soul of man for the fulfilment of his sacrifice.

Many are the significant Names by which he is addressed in the Veda. He is described as dwelling in the secret Cave, *guha*, which is used to denote the heart, *hrit*, the core of one's being. We shall choose some of the descriptive attributes which throw light on the character and function of Agni as well as the way in which he came to be worshipped in the guise of Skanda Kumara in later ages. We shall also examine some of the important passages of the Rig Veda and show how in the Mahabharata and the Puranas Agni, beyond doubt, is himself the Kumara or the latter is the Son, a manifestation of Agni.

A few references will suffice to show that the reality of Agni as God, the Immortal in the mortal, impressed the Vedic Rishis from the very beginning and is not a later development, nor the things spoken of him are applicable to the fire elemental or ritual with some fanciful deity clothed in it. The Solar powers of the sublime Truth typified by the Bhrigus are said to have brought down and placed Agni in men like a lovely treasure, for the sake of the peoples, easy to invoke. And the seer Nodhas proceeding addresses, "O Agni, Thee the Priest of the Call, the Guest worthy of choice, blissful Friend, for the Divine birth."[1] Such Riks do not give us any meaning at all, and they are numerous, unless we accept that the seers had discovered the truths of an inner existence and understood the workings of the Cosmic Powers in their progress when they embarked upon the inner voyage and knew that the immortal God from above was placed in mortal man, and that once he is awake, He, the Divine Will in man carries his offerings and leads the human soul along the Godward path to the goal. "This our sacrifice, O knower of all birth, set among the Immortals, be pleased to accept our offerings."[2] Or, hearken to Vasishtha, how easy and natural the words are: "This seer-poet, *Kavi*, the Immortal in the mortals is established among the unseeing, *akavi*;[3]

[1] .I 58.6 दधुष्ट्वा भृगवो मानुषेषु...मित्रं न शेवं दिव्याय जन्मने ।

[2] III. 21.1 इमं नो यज्ञममृतेषु धेहि इमा हव्या जातवेदो जुषस्व ।

[3] VII. 4.4 अयं कविरकविषु प्रचेताः मर्तेष्वग्निरमृतो निधायि

or again, the same Rishi in the eleventh hymn: "Thou art great, the supreme Intuition of the pilgrim-sacrifice, without thee, the Immortals are not joyous; come with all the Gods to the common chariot, here take thy seat, the first, Priest of the Call."[1] From the eighth Book let us take a verse; "To Agni, Knower of all the births, Son of Force for the gift of desirable things who becomes twofold, the Immortal in the mortals, the most delightful in the people."[2] Rishi Sauchika sings: "I saw the greatness of this great Immortal in the mortals that are the peoples".[3] In the hymns of the Atris there is a beautiful verse which speaks of the Will, the Divine Flame as shining out in the Gods, and entering with his life into the mortals.[4]* In the eleventh Sukta of the Atris we have this verse: "Fire, the supreme Intuition of the Sacrifice, the

[1] VII. 11.1 महान्नसि अध्वरस्य प्रकेतः न ऋते त्वदमृता मादयन्ते ।

[2] VIII. 71.11 अग्नि सूनुं सहसो जातवेदः...द्विता योऽभूदमृतो मर्त्येषु...

[3] X. 79.1 अपश्यमस्य महतो महित्वं अमर्त्यस्य मर्त्यासु विक्षु...

[4] V. 25.4

representative Priest, men have kindled high in the triple world of his session, let him in one chariot with Indra and the Gods take his seat on the sacred grass, the Priest of the Call, strong in will to sacrifice."[1]*

"How shall we give to Agni? For him what Word accepted by the gods is spoken, for the Lord of the brilliant plane? For him who in mortals Immortal possessed of the Truth, priest of the oblation, strongest for sacrifice, creates the gods."[2]*

"He is wide in his light like a seer of the Day; he is the one we must know and founds an adorable joy. In him is Universal life, he is the Immortal in mortals; he is the Waker in the Dawn, our Guest, the Godhead who knows all births that are."[3]*

"When man gives to Thee with the sacrifice and the fuel and with his potent words and his chants of illumination, he becomes, O Immortal, O Son of Force, a mind of knowledge among mortals and shines with the riches and inspiration and light."[4]*

[1] V. 11.2 [2] I. 77.1 [3] VI. 4.2 [4] VI. 5.5

"Fire and again Fire set to work with your fuel, chant with your speech, the dear, the beloved guest. Approach and set the immortal Light with your words; a God he enjoys in the Gods our desirable things,—a God, he enjoys our works in the Gods."[1]*

Such a God, the Immortal in us, must necessarily be somewhere in us hidden in the secrecies, in the depths of our being. The sages called it heart, *hrit*, indicated by the figure of the Cave, *guha*. Agni's dwelling place, then, is *guha* and he is so hymned by many a sage and in many a hymn in the Rig Veda. Let us give a few examples from Parashara, Vamadeva and Vishwamitra.

"He hides himself like a thief with the Cow of Vision in the secret cavern. He takes to himself our adoration and thither he carries it."[2]* Here the secret cavern, *guha*, is the core of one's being and it is still more made clear by the poet himself in another place when he says, "as the unborn he has held the wide earth, he has up-pillared Heaven with his

[1] VI. 15.6 [2] I. 65.1

mantras of Truth. Guard the cherished footprints of the Cow of Vision; O fire, thou art Universal life, enter into the secrecies of secrecies."[1]*

"He who has perceived him when he is in the secret Cave, he who has come to the stream of the Truth, those who touch the things of the Truth and kindle him,—to such a one he gives Word of the riches."[2]*

"Him in the many Mothers linked together, widespread and unapproached in the forest, abiding in the secret cave and rich with many lights, full of knowledge or moving to some unknown goal."[3]*

Again in the hymns of Vishwamitra we shall find the same *guha*, the secrécy in which he (Agni) moves (III.I.9).

Let us see how he is hymned as containing in himself the sevenfold principles of being, power, light and bliss. "The seven rays are extended in this leader of sacrifice."[4]*

"In house and house founding the seven ecstacies the Fire took its session as a priest of the Call strong for sacrifice."[5]*

[1] I. 67.3 [2] I. 67.4 [3] IV. 7.6 [4] II. 5.2 [5] V. 1.5

Or, "For me howso small impart not the heavy burden of this thought, O purifying Fire, uphold with the violence this vast profound and mighty sevenfold plane."[1]*

Vishwamitra sings: "As thy comrades we choose thee, mortals a God, for protection, Thee the Child of the Waters, the Blessed, Resplendent, the Victorious without compare."[2]

"He, Agni, Knower of the Honey, desiring the Sisters flushing red, raised them for the seeing. . . ."[3]

"Him of plenitude, the prime Intuition of the sacrifice, the priest in the front, the seven Gods of the planes adore."[4]

Again it is interesting to note that Yaska quotes a passage from the Shukla Yajurveda which plainly says, "In this body are established the seven Rishis".[5]

[1] IV. 5.6 [2] III. 9.1 सखायस्त्वा ववृमहे देवं मर्तास ऊतये...

[3] X. 5.5 सप्त स्वसॄररुषीर्वावशानो विद्वान् मध्व उज्जभारा दृशे कम्. . . .

[4] X. 122.4 यज्ञस्य केतुं प्रथमं पुरोहितं हविष्मन्त ईळते सप्त वाजिनम्..

[5] शुक्ल-यजुर्वेद. 34-55 सप्त ऋषयः प्रतिहिताः शरीरे.......

Who are the Rivers, the Waters? They are the streams of the Truth, floods of the Higher Consciousness: they are rich with the radiances of the Superconscient released by Indra, the God-mind, by slaying the Demon, the covering clouds, the obstructionist forces of Vritra that prevent the Truth-powers from entering into the Earth-consciousness. Sri Aurobindo explains the symbolism of the Waters, Rivers and Ocean by copious illustrations from the Vedic hymns. He takes up the hymns of Vasishtha (VII. 47, 49) and Vamadeva's last hymn and shows that the ocean is the image of the Infinite and eternal existence and the image of the rivers or flowing currents is used to symbolise the currents of Conscious being. And further in order to show that the Waters, the Rivers, are seven representing the seven Cosmic principles or the seven strands of being, he comments upon the first hymn of Vishwamitra to Agni from which we gather the following facts which throw light on the Puranic legends of Kumara Agni, Skanda, son of Agni born and brought up in the growths of the Earth, fostered by the sisters and moving towards his own Home, the Vast Truth.

Let us first note briefly, the relevant points. "The gods discovered Agni visible in the waters, in the workings of the sisters. The seven mighty Ones increased in him who utterly enjoys felicity; white in his birth, he is ruddy when he has grown. They moved and laboured about him, the Mares around the new-born child. The gods gave body to Agni in his birth. Wearing light as a robe about all the life of the waters he formed in himself glories vast and without any deficiency.... Here the eternal and ever young Goddesses from one womb held the one Child, they, the seven Words. Spread out were the masses of him in universal forms in the womb of the clarity, in the flowings of the sweetnesses; here the fostering rivers stood nourishing themselves. The two mothers of the accomplishing god became vast and harmonised. He discovered at his birth the source of the abundance of the Father and he loosed forth wide his streams and wide his rivers.... One, he fed upon his many mothers in their increasing. Great in the unobstructed Vast he increased; many Waters victoriously increased Agni. In the source of the Truth he lay down, there he made his home, Agni in the working of his undivided Sisters. To the visible Birth of the Waters and of the growths of Earth the goddess of Delight now gave birth in many forms, she of the utter felicity. From him increasing in the secret places of existence in his own seat within the shoreless Vast they milked out immortality."

The following extracts from Sri Aurobindo's comments are given here for the elucidation of these passages.

"These are the sevenfold waters of truth. The Divine Waters brought down from the heights of our being by Indra. It, the Divine power, is secret in the Earth's growth, *oshadhi*, the thing that holds her heats and has to be brought out by a sort of force, by a pressure of the two *aranis*, Earth and Heaven. Therefore it is called the earth's growths and the child of the earth and heaven; this immortal Force is produced by man with pain and difficulty from the workings of the pure mind upon the physical being. But in the divine waters Agni is found visible and easily born in all his strength and in all his knowledge and in all his enjoyment, entirely white and pure, growing ruddy in his action when he increases. From his very birth the gods give him force and splendour and body; the seven mighty Rivers increase him in joy. The rivers usually named *dhenavah*, fostering cows, are here described as *ashvah*, Mares, because while the Cow is the symbol of consciousness in the form of knowledge the Horse is the symbol of consciousness in the form of force, Ashva the Horse is the dynamic force of Life, and the rivers labouring over Agni on the earth become the waters of the vital dynamis or kinesis, the *prana*, which moves and acts and desires and enjoys. Agni himself begins as material heat and power, manifests secondarily as Horse and then only becomes the heavenly fire. The seven-fold waters thus rise upward and become the pure mental activity, the Mighty Ones of Heaven. They have all flowed from the one womb of the superconscient Truth—the seven Words are fundamental creative expressions of the divine Mind, *sapta vanih*. The Father of all things is the Lord and Male; he is hidden in the secret source of things, in the superconscient; Agni with his companion gods and with the seven-fold Waters, enters into the superconscient without therefore disappearing from our conscient existence, finds the source of the honeyed plenty of the father of things and pours them out on our life. He bears and himself becomes the Son, the pure Kumara, the pure Male, the One, the soul in man revealed in its universality."

V

When we ponder over the substance of these Riks of Vishwamitra with the help of Sri Aurobindo's explanation given above, it is hardly possible to miss the mystic significance that becomes quite apparent from the transparent symbols employed by the Rishi to convey the profound secrets of the divine Child, the divine Will, his birth and growth and progress to his own home in the Vast Truth. For the Rivers, the flowing Waters, the Cows, the Mares and the Child cannot be physical objects, nor cows and horses the common quadrupeds, nor can they feed a child either; much less by any stretch of imagination can rivers themselves change into fostering cows or act as mares labouring over a child. Any construing of these passages which does not admit of the symbolic imagery does necessarily involve us in imputing an insane incoherence to the mentality of these seer-poets of the ancient Vedas. It is remarkable that some of these symbolic images are preserved in the Puranas. When they say that Vishnu sleeps on the folds of the snake Ananta upon the ocean of sweet Milk, clearly they symbolise the fact that Vishnu the all-pervading God rests on the coils of the Infinite in the blissful ocean of Eternal Existence. An objection may be raised that 'that can not be really the meaning of the Purana as the priests or poets who believed that eclipses were caused by a dragon eating the sun and moon would also easily believe that the supreme Deity in a physical body went to sleep on a physical snake, upon a material ocean of real milk and that it is our own ingenuity that seeks for a spiritual meaning in these fables.' Sri Aurobindo's reply is that there is no need to seek for such meanings, for these very superstitious poets have put them plainly on the surface of the fables for everybody to see who does not choose to be blind. Mark, Vishnu means all-pervading, Ananta infinite, sweet milk a symbol of Bliss, Ananda, and Ocean, immensity of the Eternal Existence.

But the Puranic story of Skanda, Kumara the Child closely follows the Vedic account and almost keeps intact the Vedic symbolism as explained above. In the Puranas, apart from the slightly different versions, the Kumara is an effulgence of the great God, Father Shiva. He is born in the growths of the Earth, *sharavana*, placed in the Waters, Ganga, who increase him in stature; he is nourished with milk by the fostering Lights of Krittikas—in the Veda they are cows. He reaches the heights of the hill of being, the Mind Divine, called *Manasa shaila* (Mahabharata, Vanaparva, Ch. 222). He gives help to Indra, gives battle to the asuric forces, victorious, cherished and adored by the gods returns to his Father. We need not enter into the details of the story which are at every turn quite significant; but the difference between the Veda and the Purana lies in the number of the Mothers who foster him. The Veda mentions seven sisters or rivers while the Purana does only six mothers, omitting one possibly the highest height of being where fostering is not necessary.

If a doubt is entertained that we are rather ingenious in tracing the Puranic Skanda to the Vedic Kumara Agni, it vanishes if we refer to the Mahabharata in which we find a link that connects the Vedic account with that of the Puranas, notably the Skanda, Shankara Samhita among others where shorter accounts are given, as in Ramayana. There is one feature that arrests our attention while perusing the Angirasa legend followed by chapters on the birth of Kumara Skanda in the Vanaparva of the great Epic. While elaborating the story in the later Puranic way, it retains to some extent the Vedic tradition and uses certain Vedic words and names not without significance. The narrative runs from Chapter 222 to 230 in the Vanaparva. We find it plainly stated in the course of the account that Indra—God Mind—stands on the summit of the *Manasa* hill in deep contemplation waiting for the arrival of help, Agni, and that the rivers are the fostering mothers of Agni and other details which support the view that the symbolic imagery of the Vedas is maintained in the Mahabharata account of Skanda. But the most important of all is this that it refers to many forms or manifestations of Agni and names them and their functions, the last that is mentioned is called "The wonderful, *Adbhuta*" of whom the Child Kumara Skanda is a special manifestation. Here we are most concerned with this term, for there is a line here in the introduction to the story of Skanda's birth. "The greatness of Adbhuta as sung in the Vedas, I shall tell you" (221-30), says the story-teller. Now who is the Adbhuta whose greatness is praised in the Vedas? If Agni is called Adbhuta in the Vedas, then we accept without hesitation that the narrative of Skanda in the Mahabharata is based on the Vedas themselves; but ordinarily we do not know this name as specially applied to Agni, just as we know him as Purohita, placed in front or Hota, priest of the Call or Jatavedas, knower of all that is born or Saptajihva, the seven-tongued, and similar appellations that unmistakably refer to Agni. Nevertheless if we examine the texts of the Veda wherever this word occurs we find it generally applied to Agni and rarely to any other God such as Soma or Indra. Even then, when it is applied to the latter it is associated with attributes which are recognised terms for Agni. The word occurs about thirty times in the Rig Veda and in four of them in four places it is part of a compound word. Let us first be clear about the meaning of the word as it is differently given by Sayana, and then look into these passages which do not leave room for any doubt that the term Adbhuta is almost exclusively applied to Agni. Adbhuta in the Veda as in classical Sanskrit means 'wonderful', but it also means in the Veda, *mahat*, the great, Supreme, as admitted by Sayana in some places supported by Nirukta. And because it is the Supreme it transcends our comprehension, and therefore it is used in the sense of the Transcendent which is the Supreme and the Wonderful. Sri Aurobindo has translated in the sense as explained above. But what it does not and could not mean must also be stated for the sake of precision. For Sayana in some places forces it to mean 'what never was' (na bhuta, abhuta); this he does on the basis of the fantastic etymology which is abundant in Yaska's derivations of words. But the one merit of Yaska in this respect lies in the indifferent value he attaches to his explanations as is clear from the number of alternatives he light-heartedly gives to word-derivations. And Sayana quite seriously, not always, falls back upon him on occasions, when he has to tide over difficulties in explaining some phrases. '*Adbhuta-enasah*' is used as an attribute of Maruts; he explains that Maruts are Gods who are not sinful, as if other Gods were! According to him, literally, it means 'those in whom there are no sins'. Other Gods are nowhere addressed in this curious way. What seems to be the truth is this: the Maruts are known to be violent in their tempestuous action which to the mortal mind would naturally seem at times cruel as violence is and, therefore sinful; but these Maruts are Gods with wonderful sins and that is as much as to say their violence, if sin at all, is not of the ordinary kind, it is wonderful. There is a great advantage in giving the same or similar meaning to the word; it avoids the tantalising position to which we are forced quite often if we accept these unreasonable variations in the meaning. The only rational justification for this meaning of Sayana can be that even though they commit sins they are really sinless.

But our interpretation does not admit the sins at all, it holds that what appears to be violence and therefore 'sin' is not of the ordinary kind, hence wonderful, the violent action of the Maruts is wonderful. And there is another instance of a compound of which this word is a part, *adbhuta-kratu*; it can be straightly rendered 'one who has a wonderful will'. Or in Sunasshepa's Rik (1.25.1) we can easily see the word means 'wonders'; "He beholds all the wonders that have been and that have to be done".

We shall give a few instances where the Supreme is meant as the Wonderful, it is really the Transcendent that is referred to by That. "It is not now, nor is It tomorrow. Who knoweth that which is Supreme and Wonderful? It has motion and action in the Consciousness of another, but when It is approached by the thought, It vanishes."[1]* Agni is directly addressed as the Supreme or one who takes with him the Supreme. The Rishi affirms "He is the Will, he is the strength, he is the effecter of perfection, even as Mitra he becomes the charioteer of the Supreme."[2]*

"For pure understanding, I have come to the Lord of the assembly, the Wonderful, the lovable friend of Indra who gives."[3]

[1] I. 170.1 न नूनमस्ति नो श्वः कस्तद्वेद यदद्भुतम्.......

[2] I. 77.3 स हि क्रतुः.....अद्भुतस्य रथीः....

[3] I. 18.6 सदसस्पतिमद्भुतं प्रियमिन्द्रस्य काम्यम् ।
सनिं मेधामयासिषम् ।

"The bright, the purifying, the Wonderful sprinkles the sacrifice with honey."[1]

"God among Gods, Thou art friend, the Wonderful."[2]

"The King of the peoples, the Wonderful, this Agni who presides over the law I adore: may he give ear."[3]

"O Flame, Thou Supreme and Wonderful, it is Thou who by force of Will becomest in us the greatness of this discerning power; in Thee, the all-harmonising friend in the sacrifice accomplishes the work and climbs to divine mastery."[4]*

"O Flame, O Might, that rich felicity bring which shall violently overpower the armies that are embattled against us; for thou art the true in being; the Transcendent and Wonderful who gives to man the luminous plenitude."[5]*

[1] I. 142.3 शुचिः पावको अद्‌भुतो मध्वा यज्ञं मिमिक्षति...

[2] I. 94.13 देवो देवानामसि मित्रो अद्‌भुतः.....

[3] VIII. 43.24 विशां राजानमद्‌भुतं अध्यक्षं धर्मणामिमम्।
अग्निमीळे स उ श्रवत्॥

[4] V. 10.2

[5] V. 23.2

"This is the eater of the Tree for whom is poured the running butter of the Light; this is the desirable, the ancient priest of the Call, the Wonderful, the Son of Force."[1]*

"The Wonderful, the Friend propped up Earth and Heaven and made the darkness a disappearing thing by the light. He rolled out the two minds like skins; the Universal assumed every masculine might."[2]*

"The Bhrigus set in the Tree the Godhead of our aspiration with his high Flame of light like a friend well-confirmed in his place. And now, O Wonderful, well pleased in him who has cast to thee the offering, Thou art magnified by workings of thy power from day to day."[3]*

We have given those passages in which *adbhuta* is specially applied to Agni and so identified with the Supreme or said to lead to the Supreme. Even when it is occasionally used to refer to Indra the adjectives used are well-known to apply to Agni; this is evident in the Rik: "When the worshipper following

[1] II. 7.6 [2] VI. 8.3 [3] VI. 15.2

the Law and in season holds to his words of prayer he (Indra) is called the Bright, the Purifier, the Wonderful."[1] Mark the last three attributes of Agni in this verse in which Indra is addressed.

We have exhaustively given the important references to Agni as Adbhuta, an appellation which has been almost exclusively applied to him. There are solitary instances where it is applied to Indra and Soma or some other God. But this does not detract from the importance of the word mainly intended to indicate the Supreme as Agni. For it is a well-known fact that in the Veda each major God is worshipped as the Supreme, therefore the exclusive epithets of one God occasionally extend themselves to others as well. We may take the instance of hymns to Agni Vaishwanara; they always refer to the Universal Purusha, the supreme Godhead and in many Riks we find it is the Sun of Truth, Surya, as the plenary Home of Agni that is mentioned.

[1] VIII. 13.19 स्तोता यत्ते अनुव्रत उक्थान्यृतुथा दधे।
शुचिः पावक उच्यते सो अद्‌भुतः ॥

Vaishwanara, however, is primarily applied to Agni. In the light of the Angirasa legend of the Epic which mentions the Adbhuta Agni of the Vedas as the father of Skanda Kumara, and in the light of the Riks quoted above which systematically apply the term to Agni, we are entitled to conclude that the author of the Mahabharata was acquainted with the secrets of Agni as are to be discovered in the Rig Veda. This fact emerges from the unveiling of the symbols in parts in this section of the Vanaparva, identifying the Rivers and Sisters and Cows with the fostering Lights and Mothers and proceeding with its narrative in its own way but always keeping to the symbols significantly at every turn.

The significance then, of the symbolic imagery is preserved in the Puranas also, but there is a larger variation there than in the Mahabharata, at least so far as the legend of Kumara is concerned. And this fact clearly bears testimony to the correctness of our reading the hymns in their inner sense which enables us to see and appreciate their secret meaning pointing to profound truths which are clothed in the inspired words of the mystics of the Rig Veda. In this study, then, the Gods cease to be allegorical representations of mere attributes of the Godhead, but reveal themselves as substantial Realities, Powers, Personalities of the Supreme One; they are no longer personifications of mere forces of Nature, but Beings at their back and top functioning indeed in the Universe as Cosmic manifestations of the Supreme Godhead; but more intimately they are active in the inner Existence as psychological and spiritual powers with which the awakened soul enters into relation even as did the Vedic seers of yore: and of them there is One who is first to be born in man, to act as the Divine Messenger, who, while keeping himself in the front, in fact carries all the Gods in him, at the same time takes up the human soul along the path that leads to the Light, to the Truth, to Immortality —and that is the Divine Will, the Immortal in the mortal, the Flame Wonderful, *Agni Adbhuta*.

THE GODS OF THE APRI HYMNS

THE POWERS THAT FILL

THE Master, in providing us with the clues to unravel the mysteries of the Gods of the Rig Veda and of their functionings in the Universe, external and internal, has warned that the importance of a God is not to be judged by the number of hymns addressed to him, nor even by the extent of expressed invocation in the thought of the sages. This fact we have to bear in mind when we study the hymns and ponder over the functionings of the Vedic Gods. For the prominence of a God—which is not the same as the superiority of one over the others —is to be understood by such functionings of his as are immediate, direct and effective in the psychological discipline of the ancient Mystics. Looked at from this point of view, Agni, the Mystic Fire is more important than any other God of the Rig Veda, though the hymns addressed to him are less in number than those to Indra, the Lord of the Luminous Mind, the Divine Mind, the God of the third World, Swar. Agni takes a prominent, first place among the Gods of the Vedic pantheon in the outer worship and indeed plays a predominant part in the inner worship, in the Yajna. His dominance is due to his function from the very beginning in the inner being of the Rishi; for he progressively unfolds his powers assuming the forms of the other Gods or bringing their Presence to the doors of the sacrificial chamber in the inner mansions, at the altar of the awakened soul of the human being. The special character of Agni in his various functions in the inner and mystic sacrifice is nowhere so clearly and unmistakably brought to light in a concise manner as in what are called the 'Apri Hymns'. In this short study, we propose to think out the full implications of the term '*āpri*' and the significance of the Riks of the hymns that has bearing on the advent of other Gods or their manifestation in the progression of the well-kindled Agni in the onward march of the Aryan soul in the inner sacrifice.

Before proceeding to consider the nature of the Apri hymns, let us briefly recount the All-inclusive functions of Agni in the Rig Veda. Agni is the principle of heat and light in the external nature, a principle by which all developments of forms and renewal of forms, and purification in a general way are made possible. But Agni, in the spiritual and psychological discipline of the Vedic mystic, while not excluded from his external functioning in the world, takes an intimate place in the inner life that leads to the Light supernal, the Immortal Life, the supreme Truth-Consciousness above. For though the Highest Truth, the Supreme Consciousness is present everywhere in the universe, its plenary Home is above and beyond the triple world of ours, termed in the Vedic parlance, *Bhūh*, represented by Matter, the gross physical, *Bhuvah*, the mid-air region dominated by the principle of Life-force and *Swar*, the luminious pure mind of the higher Consciousness. Agni's function is of course varied in the outer universe but is not confined to that, it continues in the inner universe of man to build it up and effect the development of the Cosmic Powers in him for the perfection that makes for his competency to attain the Truth-Light and Immortality. The fundamental nature of Agni is that he is the Divine Will that is at work in the Universe. Since he is the Divine Will, his true Home is the Home of Truth above the Mind-world in the Swar. Since Creation proceeds from above downwards he comes down to Earth and functions in the gross existence as the fire that assimilates the *rasa*, the sap in things, that is to say, the essence of their substantial being, he is also the Will in the dynamic life-energy, *prāna*. Thus gradually his function advances from the physical to the psychological and spiritual nature of human existence. For Agni is born in man and ascends, he transfigures his powers into the energies of mind. And when Agni burns, 'our passions and emotions are the smoke of his burning. Our nervous forces are assured of their action only by the support' of this mystic Fire, Agni.

Now we can appreciate without difficulty the prime place occupied by Agni in the Godward path of the Vedic sages. For when human aspiration rises towards the utmost possible perfection, when man strives for a divine birth and divine fulfilment, when the human soul has developed itself to such an extent as to give itself willingly to the Great In-dweller and with trust in the Divine Will and when to do this he is ripe and gets the strength and courage, when he is thus definitely on the way through devotion and arduous discipline, *tapasyā*, and a confident knowledge of and faith in the higher Powers that transcend his many-sided limitation, then is the hour for the awakening of the human soul to the active presence of Agni, the Divine Will at work within him; then is he fit to perform the self-giving, the sacrifice called Yajna, the true worship.

When Agni, the Seer-Will, *Kavikratu*, is awakened in the human being, when he is well-kindled, fostered and enabled to increase in volume and intensity, many developments take place until finally and fully the Divine flame takes charge of the whole being of man in his journey upwards to the regions of the Gods above that border on the Home of the

Eternal Truth, the undying Light. But this charge of Agni is effective and takes place when the utter self-giving symbolised by the ritual of animal sacrifice, *pashumedha*, is accomplished. And for this achievement of the true sacrifice of self-giving, many Higher powers have to extend their help to the sacrificer, *yajamāna*, through the summonings of Agni who is already awakened and interested, though not yet in full charge of the task for the fulfilment of the work. This preliminary stage is a definite step to come face to face with the higher powers of Agni himself or through his intervention to commune with the Cosmic Powers of a higher existence. It is at this point that the Rishi prays for the help of the higher Powers manifested in Agni who develops out of his own body of Divine Truth and substance the Gods of the higher realms or calls them down to be present in him, for the effective march of the sacrifice, for assisting the Rishi to give his full support to the workings so that in this sense they may be born in him, and he be taken up into them.

These prayers are called Apri hymns. The term can be interpreted in two ways. Ordinarily, it is taken to mean that they propitiate and are pleasing to the Gods, *ā-prīnayantyah*, otherwise termed technically *yājyāh*, *stutayah*, laudatory verses. But *āpriyah* is justly derived from *pri* to fill, as Sayana himself does in (II.6.8.): *chikitvah sa vidwān a cha piprayah*, 'such art Thou the Conscious Fire, *fill* us'. And in this case especially in the inner worship or sacrifice these higher Powers of Agni, i.e., the Gods, are addressed to come down and *fill* the Rishi. While the Apri hymns are used in the ritual as a preliminary to the animal sacrifice, its significance in the inner life of the Rishi is quite clear in that it invokes the help and presence of the Gods whose advent is vouchsafed to the Rishi by the progressive unfoldment of the powers of Agni himself. In every Mandala of the Rig Veda we have Apri hymns, except in the fourth, sixth and eighth. There has been a systematic arrangement of the verses of these hymns and usually they are eleven or twelve, occasionally thirteen verses in an Apri hymn.

The Powers, *devatās*, addressed are all of Agni origin; therefore they are included in the hymns to Agni. In ancient times, as Yaska remarks, there was divergence of opinion in regard to the Devatas of these hymns. Some held that Yajna itself as a Person, *purusha*, is the Deity and they gave their reasons; some held Agni himself to be the Deity with sufficient reason. But the real difficulty in determining the Devata of some of the verses is that, Indra, Twashtr, the three Goddesses, Ila, Saraswati and Bharati and others are mentioned in these hymns. Ordinarily their functions differ from those of Agni. But the difficulty is not very real; for Agni himself, in his progress in the inner life of the Rishi, assumes the forms of the other Gods. This development is a special feature of Agni. For it is characteristic of him to become in his heavenward activity endowed with attributes that distinguish severally the other Gods of the Vedic system, while retaining his distinguishing feature of the Divine Will that is initially born as the Flame of human aspiration to the Sublime. This description of Agni appearing as different Gods is a general feature of the Vedic hymns and it is so expressed in clear terms in certain Riks also. When Agni is born, there is an encompassing wideness, that is because of his Varuna aspect. When he is well-kindled, he becomes the Lord of love and friendship. So says Rishi Vasushruta of the Atri house. Let us quote here two of the verses from Sri Aurobindo's translation of a hymn which brings to the fore the truth of what we have stated in regard to the multiple Divine Personality of Agni.

> "Thou art he of the Wideness, O Will, when thou art born; thou becomest the Lord of Love when thou art entirely kindled. In thee are all the gods, O Son of Force; thou art the Power-in-Mind for the mortal who gives the offering.
>
> "O thou who possessest self-ordering Nature, thou becomest the might of the Aspirer when thou bearest the secret Name of the Virgins. They brighten thee with

> the Light in her rays as Love perfectly founded when thou makest of one mind the Lord and his Spouse in their mansion." (Rig Veda V.3, 1-2)

Such is the magnificent character of the Divine Will when it is awakened and set to work in the system of the human being. But here a difference must be noted between Agni as Varuna, Mitra, Aryaman and others as mentioned in the verses quoted above, and Agni as bringing about the advent of his higher powers from above for the fulfilment of the Rishi's aspiration. There it is shown in a general way that Agni is in reality and ultimately all the other gods. Here in the Apri hymns, the powers of Agni are invoked, step by step, for certain functions direct and limited and immediate; some of them are Gods of the higher worlds and planes of Consciousness, while others are a sort of personification, so to say, of the manifestations of Agni himself here on the earth-plane, in the inner consciousness of the Rishi. Thus we find in these hymns the Doors that are called upon to open heavenwards are addressed as deities. The offerings of small pieces of wood that feed the flame to grow, are called deities; also there are other well-known Gods and Goddesses whose functions are clearly defined and recognised; and they too are included in the Apri for the simple reason that their functioning is indispensable for the fulfilment of the preliminary step, the step that immediately precedes the consummation of the inner worship, the sacrifice by which Agni himself takes the full responsibility and charge of the entire task of the human soul embarking on the heavenward voyage. We shall presently take up a short Apri hymn for example in which reference to these manifestations of Agni is made unmistakably, using the same appellation for the Deity concerned; and all the Rishis who sing the Apri hymns are of one voice and the order and arrangement of the deities are generally the same with very few variations. For the Rishis of these Apri hymns come from different houses and while adopting the technique common to all of them—for the principle was recognised and received universal acceptance among the mystics—they varied slightly the formula of including certain deities which are otherwise done by the Rishis of different houses. Thus, for instance, in the place of *tanūnapat* which means child of the body, they address *Narāshamsa*, one who speaks out the Gods. Some Apris include both of them. Another small difference among the Apris is that the major Gods like Indra are mentioned in some and left out in others. But everywhere the same important Powers or deities are invoked which throw a flood of light on the mystic passage that led the Rishi from here on Earth while living in the physical body to the heavenward road in which communion with the higher Cosmic Powers was made possible while arriving at the ultimate goal of the Supreme Truth, the sole Godhead.

Let us take a hymn in a short metre, illustrative of the character of the Apri hymn, choosing from the Apris which are ten in all, found in the various books of the Rik Samhita.

The Apri of Medhatithi Kanwa (RV. 1.13.) contains twelve Riks in Gayatri metre and is enough for our purpose which is to show how the Flame of the Divine Will is invoked to effect step by step the advent of his own higher Powers and those of the high existence for the uplift of the aspiring soul through the means of utter self-offering—the consummate worship, the true sacrifice—Yajna.

1. Well-kindled, O Agni, do thou bring the Gods for me, equipped with sacred offerings. O Summoner, Purifier, perform the worship.[1]

The Rishi addresses Agni. He is already awakened from his slumber by the single-willed aspiration of the Rishi, by proper initiation, by *tapasyā* and mystic discipline. This awakening is the birth in man of the Divine Will as distinct from the human will. But it has to be tended and fostered with care and vigilance. The Flame is to be fed

[1] RV. 1. 13
सुसमिद्धो न आ वह देवाँ अग्ने हविष्मते ।
होतः पावक यक्षि च ॥१॥

by the fuel, the *samit* of devotional prayers backed by an exclusive choice of the Divine by the human will. Thus, well kindled, *susamiddha*, he, the Divine Flame is enabled to rise high enough to bring the Gods of the higher realms for the sacrifice. But he will not and cannot bring them for one who keeps to himself what belongs to the Gods and therefore to be offered to them. Therefore for me, for one who has kept ready the offerings to make, *havishmate*, bring the Gods, it is said. Agni, the Divine Flame is also the Divine Voice, therefore he is the Summoner who calls the Gods and his Call is effective there where the human cry and call do not reach. He is thus addressed as *Hotar*, Caller. Still he has to function in the human vessel, which in the best among men retains elements of impurity that clogs and limits and disfigures the higher functionings of the new-born Flame. Purification, then, is necessary, and this Agni himself effects in the human being. For only to a tolerably pure Adhar, the human vessel, the Gods can be expected to come. So, he is *pāvaka*, purifier. When the Gods come, worship is to be offered to them. The human being does not know how to receive and respect and use a language that can please the Gods. So Agni himself is called upon to do the worship. As *sacrifice* was the ceremonial form that congregational worship in the ancient times assumed, *Yajna* came to mean sacrifice. Therefore we shall translate Yajna equivocally as true worship or sacrifice which does not mean in our sense of the word in the context, goat-immolation or any other animal slaughter.

2. Child of the Body, O Seer, do perform this our sacrifice to the Gods, fraught with the Honey of Soma-Wine, for the purpose of their advent.[1]

The Rishi now calls upon Agni, Child of the body to give form to the sacrifice, i.e., to accomplish the worship to the Gods on

[1] मधुमन्तं तनूनपाद्यज्ञं देवेषु नः कवे।
अद्या कृणुहि वीतये ॥२॥

his behalf. *Tanūnapat*, can mean child born of the body of Agni which is the Flame in which case he is a manifestation, a special form of the Divine Flame as it increases in volume, stature and intensity. So the term is a recognised appellation to Agni even in classical Sanskrit. But it can mean child born of the body of the sacrificer, *yajamāna*, in whom the Flame of the Divine Will is born and thus the *tanūnapat* is none other than the well-kindled Agni referred to in the first Rik, but the appellation here is significant in that it brings out the close relation, the intimacy that is developed between the Divine flame and the earnest worshipper. Because he is so intimate, the Rishi implores that he may be pleased to formulate the sacrifice, to give a definite shape to it among the Gods, *yajnam krinuhi deveshu*. And he is addressed as Kavi, seer; for he sees and knows the way to reach the worshipper's offerings to the Gods. And the sacrifice, the Yajna, is fraught with the Honey, the honey of the Soma Wine which represents the outflowing of the principle of Delight in things.

The human being that has launched upon the sublime worship of utter sacrifice, the giving of itself and all that belongs to it, offers the Soma, the *rasa*, the sap of all experiences of Delight in things and thus Soma is, indeed, the soul of all Yajna, *madhumantam*; it is for the offering of this *rasa*, all preparations are made, all the preliminary steps are taken with great care. The Yajna, then, is filled with this honey for the acceptance of the Gods who are to come down at the fervent call of *tanūnapat* on behalf of the worshipper. Without the *madhu*, this honey, there is no purpose in calling the Higher Powers for the sacrifice. When the *madhu* is there, the advent of the Gods is assured, *vītaye*. It must be noted that *vīti* means at once eating, *bhakshana*, as well as coming down, *āgamana*. In the ceremonial worship, it means they are called to eat the honey. In the inner worship, they are invoked for their advent or manifestation at the sacrifice.

3. Beloved Narashamsa, sweet-tongued, who prepares the sacred offering, I call upon

in this sacrifice.[1]

Narāshamsa is Agni who voices the Godhead. For Nara in the Veda means the Gods, though it may mean men also; strength is the element that is common to both. The strong male Gods are leaders, called *narāḥ*. Now the Divine Child born in the sacrificer has endeared himself to him, and is ready and willing to do the needful; he is beloved, *priya*. He is sweet-tongued, *madhu-jihva*; the rising flame is the tongue of Agni; when it goes up high enough, it touches and reaches the Gods, carrying with it as it does, something of the taste, the agreeable sweet of the sacrifice that draws the Gods to it who respond to the offering naturally with a spontaneity that is characteristic of Divine response to the fervent prayers of man. And the offering itself is well prepared and accomplished by Agni, *narāshamsa* himself; for however arduous may be the discipline followed by the ardent

[1] नराशंसमिह प्रियमस्मिन्यज्ञ उप ह्वये ।
मधुजिह्वं हविष्कृतम् ॥३॥

worshipper, whatever the care and zeal and the human wisdom at its best that attend the human perfection, it can not equal the wisdom of the Divine flame when it is allowed to undertake the task of preparing the offering itself in order to carry it to perfection. Thus he is *havishkrit*. Such is the Divine flame who voices the Godhead and he is invoked now to come close and be present at the Yajna. Thus it will be seen that he is quite a natural aspect of Agni, not a special manifestation or any of the other Gods.

4. Agni, aspired to (by us), on thy most happy car bring the Gods hither; Manu has fixed thee as the Summoner.[1]

Agni is now invoked in his central aspect of *īdita* or *īlita*, one who is aspired to and invoked to be the officiant appointed with due respect to conduct the sacrifice. *Id* or *Il*, the root means, according to ancient authorities

[1] अग्ने सुखतमे रथे देवान् ईळित आ वह।
अंसि होता मनुर्हितः ॥४॥

like Yaska, to praise, to worship or to beg. And in this last sense, the sense of aspiration is implied and is so translated by Sri Aurobindo. And in Sanskrit it is *adhyeshanā* which technically means an act in which a God or a respected person is called upon with due reverence to fulfil a function. Now *īdita* Agni has to appear and when he so does, it is not a quiet seeing or raising his voice to the Gods, he comes in a happy movement; dynamic is he and his advent in the car brings a most rapid and happy movement, *sukhatama ratha*, in which he is to bring the Gods. It is his car, his rapid movement that is charged with the advent of the Higher Powers.

How or why does he do it? Here the third foot of the Rik gives the answer; at the same time it reveals a secret which has much to do with the mystic discipline of the Vedic seers. He is the *hotā*, the summoning priest who calls the Gods, and to this position he is appointed, that is to say, he is fixed to this function by Manu, *manurhitaḥ*. Manu, says Sayana, is Mantra, though he gives an alternative meaning of *manushya*, man, who is the sacrificer. Though both are intelligible in the context, the first meaning, i.e. the *mantra* is more appropriate and reveals the fact that the mantra, the inspired and revelatory Word has gone forth from the supreme Ether, *paramam vyoma*, to fix the Divine Flame in the Rishi, to carry out the great work of sacrifice and it is that sublime Voice, the *Vāk*, the Mantra that the Initiate employed in establishing the Flame in him and keeping the entire task to the trust and care of the Divine Caller. This is the gist of the last line of the Rik.

It may be mentioned here that the word *manu* is employed to denote *mantra* in the Tantra Shastra and is a technical term, so understood even today.

The alternate meaning as suggested by Sayana is harmless and does not require elucidation, as the sacrificer is supposed to employ Agni in the ceremonial rite to officiate as the priest who calls upon the Gods to be present and accept the offerings at the sacrifice.

5. O Ye Wise Ones, spread the seat of sacred

grass of bright surface, in unbroken order where the Immortal is beheld.[1]

It is usual with the hymnodists of the Rig Veda to resort quite often to address themselves i.e. to the inner self, or to call upon comrades who are engaged in the Yajna. It is a general way of expressing themselves as to what they are persuaded to do or persuade their following to observe. Here the Rishi addresses the wise ones, *manīshinaḥ.* The next step to be proceeded upon is to keep ready the seat for the Gods of whom Agni is the first in order to take his place at the altar. The sacred grass, *barhiḥ*, is the symbol used in the ritual to prepare the seat. It is to be spread, *stṛnīta*, in due form, in unbroken order, *ānushak*, well-prepared and close so that every part of the seat will reveal its relation to the whole to be occupied by the Gods in regular order that starts with Agni. The seat is indeed within the inner being of man. It must not be supposed that it is a

[1] स्तृणीत बर्हिरानुषग्घृतपृष्ठं मनीषिणः ।
यत्रामृतस्य चक्षणम् ॥५॥

point or some imagined spot or heart in the physical frame of the human being. The seat for the Gods is indeed within, in the inner being which is wider and far greater and subtler, and supple and enlightened and distinguished from the physical being. We have to speak of it as within because the outer self and the outgoing mind and vital activities are all but a modicum of that larger being behind and even encompassing them. Once the initiation into the secret path that leads to the inner chamber takes effect, the outer normal self of man with all its thinkings and doings dwindles into a nothing before the wideness at the threshold of the vast Self within in which the sacred seat of Gods is arranged for the welcome of the Higher Powers.

But the seat must be kept pure and bright; this is effected by the clarities of the mind and heart of the Rishi, so that at first sight, on the very surface it is splendid enough to be god-inviting, *ghrita-prishtha.* Such a state of purity in the inner apartment glittering with the clarity of clear perception of the heart, is adorable and is the right condition for the Godhead to reveal himself. So, the Rishi says, there in that holy seat, the Immortal is beheld, *amritasya chakshanam*. Here the Immortal is Agni himself; he can be clearly seen as the Immortal Godhead himself. He, the Rishi, may have felt him as the Divine Will different from his willings and strivings; he may have received from him the necessary guidance and help in his disciplinary exertions; he may have even had an assured contact of some kind in his laudable enterprise, but to behold him as the Immortal is different from all these things. Now in the sacred hall at the altar, in the Vast field of the inner being bright with the brightness of clarity, he, the Immortal is beheld. Such is the sanctity of the seat of sacred grass arranged and regulated in position, in uninterrupted sequence.

Till now, the Rishi invoked Agni himself as one Well-kindled, *susamiddha*, as child born of the body, *tanūnapat*, as one who voices the Godhead, *narāshamsa*, and as the very seat sacred for the advent of the Gods, *barhiḥ*. For, the ancient tradition that Barhih is a name worn by Agni, has meaning for us in the esoteric interpretation for the simple reason that the *barhiḥ* as described in this Rik can be nothing else but the result of the workings of Agni, an indispensable manifestation of the Divine Flame in the human being.

6. May the splendorous (or Divine) Doors truth-increasing, swing open, that do not stick up close, for the sacrifice now and sure.[1]

Now the next step, mentioned in this Rik, is a revelation of the character of Yajna as also of the ancients' mastery of the intricacies that beset the passage of the Vedic Yoga. The Rishi now calls upon the Doors to open that ordinarily are closed to mortals in their ignorant strivings. What are these doors that are called upon to open and what for? The Yajna, in the common conception of the Rishis, is to be treated as something definite and well-shaped, and it proceeds upwards;

[1] वि श्रयन्तामृतावृधो द्वारो देवीरसश्चतः ।
अद्या नूनं च यष्टवे ॥६॥

yajnam urdhwam kuruta, is a phrase we often meet with in the Rik Samhita itself, not to speak of the Brahmanas and kindred literature. Now the Yajna has to rise and travel heavenward to reach ultimately the Godhead; but as it goes up it reaches the realms of the Gods who come down to the sacrificer's chamber; thus the passage is to be made clear, the Doors that lead upwards which are usually closed, must open for the sacrifice and therefore for the sacrificer. These doors are not obscure or somewhere vaguely above, elsewhere in the dark; when there is so much preparation and fitness on the part of the human aspirant and the seat within him for the Gods is made ready for the Gods, and he can behold the undying Flame within him, he is fully qualified to see the Doors that open upwards; for they too are shining, splendorous, *devīr dvārah*. They are not there always to remain closed to all; they are there to swing wide open for the mortal who is qualified and seeks the Immortal. *Vishrayantām*, may they swing open, says the Rik. When they open, they increase the truth to the vision of the seer and to that extent it increases in him, *ritāvridhā*. The very appearance of the doors shining is an assurance that there are higher truths and their Powers beyond which are visible when the doors open. Thus they are increasers of Truth, in the sense that the Truth begins to grow larger and larger to the vision of the seeker at the sight of the opening of the Divine Doors, not that the Doors in any way affect the Truth as it is; and increasing the Truth in any other sense is an absurdity. They are not hard to open themselves, for they are not close stuck up and obstinate, *asaschatah*, but ever waiting to make way and show the passage for the Sacrifice, for the sacrificer, for the Divine Flame, for all the higher Powers of the ultimate Godhead—and all this through the intervention of the new-born Immortal child in the mortal man. Let the Doors be open for passage of the sacrifice, *yashtave*.[1]

[1] It may be mentioned that the opening of the Doors in the Yoga of the Vedic Mystics corresponds to the opening of the psycho-physical centres (*chakra-bheda*) in the Yogic systems of latter ages that have attempted to preserve something of the esoteric wisdom in the Vedic lore. Stress is laid on the Divine Will and the Divine

7. Night and Dawn of auspicious form, I invoke to seat them on the sacred grass at this our solemn worship (sacrifice).[1]

In the mystic discipline of these ancient sages, there are alternations of Day and Night both of which are equally important for the perfect fulfilment of the purpose of sacrifice. It must be noted that the Day and Night are symbols in the esoteric system of the Vedic sages, of the alternations of the Divine and human consciousness in us. The Night of our ordinary Consciousness, says Sri Aurobindo, holds and prepares all that the Dawn brings out into conscious being. Day also in another way represents broad open light, the light of Consciousness in which the worlds and planes and their Powers are beheld severally and in toto, while Night represents a concentration and self-absorption in the con-

Powers in the Vedic path while in the latter and Tantric systems stress falls on personal effort.

[1] नक्तोषासा सुपेशसास्मिन् यज्ञ उप ह्वये।
इदं नो बर्हिरासदे ॥७॥

sciousness, an intensity of self-gathering in what we may call the immobile, static existence in which there is nothing else to be seen, but in which the all is absorbed; the Truths, the planes and their Powers and the Gods and all beings and things lie latent and hidden and seem to be non-existent, as it were. Such alternation in the consciousness was a necessity in the mystic discipline of the Rishis for the perfection towards Immortality that was their aim. Hence Day and Night, *nakta-ushāsa*, of distinct auspicious forms, *supeshasā*, are called upon to be present. Though this seems to be a personification of day and night as deities, the idea is clear in the mind of the Rishi that both the states must be made possible for him in his endeavour. The Day-consciousness shall not dazzle him and make him forgetful of the Night in whose womb lies the Day. The significance of invoking both together which are apparently of different hues, white and black, and can never co-exist lies in the fact that in the Vedic Yoga both are equally important and be made familiar to the being of the Rishi in whom both the forms, the twin sisters, Day and Night—can abide. It is this twin aspect of the Consciousness with necessary variation in its connotation that is the origin and support of the dictum of the Upanishad that both 'Knowledge and Ignorance' must be known together. 'He who knows That as both in one, the Knowledge and the Ignorance, by the Ignorance crosses beyond death and by the Knowledge enjoys Immortality.' We may note in passing that this concept of Day and Night is expressed figuratively in the famous passage of the Gita that what is day to the Wise is night to the common man and *vice versa*. The Isha Upanishad text quoted above clearly says with reference to the Knowledge and Ignorance and Birth and non-birth, to be known together, that 'we have heard it from the Wise ones of yore.' Who else could these Wise ones be but the mystics of the Vedic Wisdom, *Dhīrāḥ*?

This, then, is the significance of the Rishi's invocation to the Day and the Night to be present at the sacrifice and take their places in the seat made ready for the advent of the Gods to the sacrificial Hall in the inner

Mansion of the larger and wider being of the Rishi.

8. I invite the twin Divine Priests of the Call, sweet-tongued, Seers; let them conduct the worship at the sacrifice.[1]

Hitherto the Agni Powers were invoked, and the Divine Doors were addressed to swing open wide and with so much of equipment, the Rishi addresses himself to settle in a position in which both the Divine Consciousness and human consciousness can be held together, or the static and dynamic aspects of the Consciousness as described in the note on the previous Rik can be contained in his being. The next step, then, is to invite the help of the Powers above the Earth-plane, though they have been at work in a general way all along without palpable distinction. Now the Rishi calls upon the two Divine Priests of the Call, *daivyā hotārā*, who are Cosmic Powers on the

[1] ता सुजिह्वा उप ह्वये होतारा दैव्या कवी।
यज्ञं नो यक्षतामिमम् ॥८॥

Plane of the mid-air regions, of the world of Life-powers. They are seers, *kavi*. Now they are called upon to conduct the sacrifice. It is true that Agni as a matter of fact is in entire charge of the Sacrifice and that is a general function, but the distinct Powers are to manifest themselves and take their places and play their parts. And who are these Divine Priests of the Call? What is our authority to state with certainty or even to suppose that they dwell in the *Bhuvarloka*, the world of Vayu or Prana, the Life-World? There is nothing in this Rik to show that they are so, although we are entitled to surmise that their normal place is just above the Earth-plane, mentioned as they are after the invocation to the Divine Doors that swing open upon the Higher worlds through which the Yajna is to journey towards the Realm of the Ultimate Reality—the Supreme Godhead, the Sun of Truth. There is authority, not mere surmise. For in other Apri hymns, they are described as the two Divine Priests of the Call for our humanity, *manusho daivyā hotārā*, and are called upon to come on the paths of the Life-breath, *vāyoh patmanā*. They are the first *prathamā*, full in wisdom and stature, *vidushtarā vapushtarā*. They are divine by nature, divine in stature and have a happy tongue, *sujihvā*, that speaks what is good and auspicious to man; they are the God-appointed heralds whose voice is pleasing to the Gods when it functions for the rise of humanity.

But we have no clues here in this hymn or in other Apris to discover the significance of the two. Here we have to fall back upon what may appear to be conjecture. The two may represent the upward movement that reaches the subtle higher planes of the Gods and the downward movement that brings down the higher powers and something of the substance of the higher worlds to the human being engaged in the sacrifice. Since they are always addressed in twain, it can also be the twin powers of Light and Life fixed in the mid-world to call upon the Gods to come down for the sake of humanity of which they are the appointed priests of the Call.

9. Ila, Saraswati, Mahi, three Goddesses,

delight-producers—may they be seated, unassailed, on the sacred grass-seat.[1]

We have now reached a step where there is a direct reference in unmistakable terms to three distinct Powers that are open to the aspiring soul. They afford an indispensable basis, quite tangible to the developing human consciousness that is released from the crampings and closings of crowded thoughts and feelings in the ignorance and darkness that stamp the common run of life; for the ordinary man is not turned Godwards, not wedded to the giving of himself to the Gods, Intelligent Powers of the Cosmic Godhead. What are these three Powers? They are, of course, the three well-known Goddesses of the Vedic Yoga; they are Shaktis, powers from the Home of the Vast, the Sun of Truth, *ṛtam jyotir bṛhat*. Their names are sufficiently indicative of their functions; for Ila is the Goddess of the vision of Knowledge; Saraswati. is she

[1] इळा सरस्वती मही तिस्रो देवीर्मयोभुवः।
बर्हिः सीदन्त्वस्रिधः ॥९॥

of its flowing Inspiration; Bharati is the Goddess of its Vastness, the vastness of the Truth. Here in this Rik, Bharati is not mentioned by name, but referred to by an attribute which means the great *mahī*, which is the same as *mahatī* or *bṛhatī* and Bharati means she of the Bharata, Aditya, the Sun of Truth. Indeed she is the Power of vastness who takes the first place in the trinity of Goddesses though mentioned last in the order; and when she appears and removes the narrowness of the little human stuff, a wideness and vastness in, around and above opens upon man, accompanied by the vision of Knowledge, Ila, and Saraswati, the Inspiration that expresses the truth-knowledge and truth-vision in vocal terms. These three Powers are inestimable for the Rishi who has launched the great ship of Sacrifice in the charted sea of the hierarchy of Planes, of the rising tier of level after level of being, so that it may not flounder anywhere losing the way. Once they bestow their favour upon the Rishi at the opening of the Divine Doors, he feels a happiness, has the joy of bliss on the way, for they give birth to delight, *mayobhuvah.* There is no fear of fall or failing in the midway, for they are not attacked by Ignorance and darkness, *asridhah,* to which are due all human sorrows and sufferings. The vision and inspiration and presence of the Vast are unfailing and the steps to be taken forward are assured of their rectitude and are straight and effective throughout the passage.

It is these three Goddesses that are called upon to take their seats at the altar, strewn of Grass, the symbolic character of which has been explained in the note on an earlier Rik.

10. I invoke Twashtr, the excellent (or the foremost), the author of all forms. May he be our sole (adored God).[1]

Now Twashtr is addressed. For he is the fashioner of all things in creation; as such he is the foremost *agriya* in giving shape to things and forms of beings in the Cosmos. Therefore his are all forms, *vishwa-rūpa.* Twashtr therefore has to confer upon the aspiring Aryan

[1] इह त्वष्टारमग्रियं विश्वरूपमुप ह्वये।
अस्माकमस्तु केवल: ॥१०॥

in the Yajna, his favours which build the new life, give new shape to the old material in the human being, remove the elements that are obstinate or change them to suit his purpose for the fashioning of the substance in the human being that could answer to the demands of the higher laws, the laws of the Divine Powers; for it is their manifestation in the human being that requires adequate response and a fit condition in the mortal frame of man for utilisation and proper adjustment. Here the importance of Twashtr in the new construction or resuscitation of the old structure of the human being cannot be exaggerated. Therefore to stress the function of Twashtr, the Rik adds, 'may he be our Absolute,' *kevalah*. It means, in other words, the sole and adored God.

11. O Lord of the Earth's growths, thou art God and to the Gods offer this our oblation. May there be the tangible Knowledge to the giver.[1]

[1] अव सृजा वनस्पते देव देवेभ्यो हविः ।
प्र दातुरस्तु चेतनम् ॥११॥

Then there is the invocation to Soma. He is addressed as the Lord of Plants, of the Earth's growths, *vanaspati*. He is called upon to offer the oblation to the Gods. The significance of Soma, the lord of delight in things, being called upon to offer the oblation lies in the fact that the outflowing of *rasa*, the principle of delight in the human being, is absolutely essential in all worship to the Gods; a dry heart, a creature in depression can never rise above the common human level at its lowest, and whatever offering is made and prayers are offered, cannot reach the Gods; they go to feed and fatten the wrong elements, the adverse forces, the Pishacha, and the Rakshasa. It is only a glad heart and joyous feeling that can nourish a happy trust backing the offerings and prayers leading to self-giving. Thus Soma is mentioned for the purpose of making sure to one's self the joyous element in the offering. When such a holy gift is made in the proper way, the result cannot be mistaken and the Rishi makes bold to say, 'Let the giver be blessed with tangible Knowledge,' *chetanam*. Hitherto there has been invocation to the Powers. Now the essential thing asked for is consciousness. It is not a mental thought, however illumined it may be or a sort of knowledge based upon it; but an indubitable knowledge, a consciousness in which what is known is felt and tangible and *chetana* means, as the root even in classical Sanskrit is understood, *sam-jnāna*, contactual knowledge i.e., higher consciousness that is in close contact with the senses and sense-mind. The Rishi prays for such a substantial knowledge in which doubt has no place and certitude is dominant.

12. With Swaha offer the sacrifice to Indra in the house of the worshipper, I call the Gods thither.[1]

Now the closing Rik of the hymn mentions the purpose of the Sacrifice. Here there is no invocation to any God, but there is a call to the friends, others engaged in the sacred

[3] स्वाहा यज्ञं कृणोतनेन्द्राय यज्वनो गृहे।
तत्र देवान् उप ह्वये ॥१२॥

toil, as in an earlier Rik. It must be borne in mind that all sacrifice is undertaken to arrive at the Lord of Swar, Indra, the Divine Mind. For he is the Lord of the triple world of ours, and the King of Gods *devarāja*; above him, i.e., beyond the triple world is the Sun of Truth with which as a matter of course he is in touch—and he himself is a sublime manifestation of That,—the Truth which is not directly related to this triple world in the Ignorance. Therefore Indra is the chief God to whom the Soma is offered. Swaha is a sacred utterance used to appeal to the Gods when offerings are given and request made for their acceptance. 'To Indra offer the sacrifice with Swaha,' says the Rik.

Where is the sacrifice conducted? In the house of the sacrificer, *yajvano grihe*. Certainly this house of the *yajvan* is his own body with life and mind alive to their functions. The Rishi proclaims with confidence that he would call the other Gods there; for the King of the Gods is not to come alone; others, his assistants, the Powers are necessarily to attend upon him, *tatra devan upahvaye*.

Thus closes the Apri hymn of Medhatithi Kanva. This is the simplest of Apri hymns chosen here to show that there has been a methodical arrangement of the Riks in these hymns which are employed in the rite preliminary to the main sacrifice. But in the inner sacrifice, as has been shown, they are addressed to the Powers that come down and fill, *āpūrayitryaḥ*, the Rishi, the sacrificer, making him fit to execute the utter self-giving that is the meaning of Yajna. Even a casual reading of these hymns, without much scrutiny or close study will make it clear to the intelligent mind that on the very surface the Powers that are invoked, and accompanied by others are always the one well-kindled, the child born of the body or the one that voices the Godhead, the seat at the Altar, the Doors Divine, the two Divine Priests of the Call, the three Goddesses—and these are all systematically mentioned and their functionings are unequivocal in their order, while the other Powers that are mentioned may vary with the hymns; and this variance is negligible and does not alter the character of the Apri. The

Apri, thus, is a clear indication of the mysteries of the Vedic Yoga followed by the *seers* of ancient times, marked by ordered steps with definite purpose at each stage in their journey towards the Home of Utter Bliss, the Immortal Life, the Truth Eternal.

ANJAH-SAVA
OR
THE RAPID RITE OF A SEER-PRIEST

As we follow in the footsteps of the Master in our studies of the hymns of the Rig Veda, we get more and more convinced not merely of the straightforwardness of the approach that leads us to discover the inner and true sense of the Riks, but of another fact. It is the conviction growing upon us that this is the only true way, that the inner meaning is the substance which is the treasure of spiritual wisdom and Knowledge of the Gods and the Godhead. It is not that there is nothing else, any more or less than this, it may contain within it concealed other knowledge that pertains to the domain of many branches of Science. There may be and is room for other line or lines of approach affording fields of thought, for those interested in Astronomy,

Geology, Biology or Ayurveda. But the one inner meaning that runs consistently through the whole body of the hymnal text is the main issue of the Veda and that is the spiritual and occult knowledge and Divine Wisdom which certainly justifies the hoary tradition of India among all religions and sects and saints that the Veda is Revelation and Divine Scripture. It may throw light on other objects of Knowledge, but they are side-issues, not the main spirit and substance which is knowledge of truths about the Godhead and the Gods who are Powers and Personalities of the Godhead and about their status and manifestation in the Cosmos as well as in man.

Apart from this sacred tradition which is based upon the secret and inner sense of the Veda, there runs a parallel tradition that the Veda is a book of Works, *Karma Kanda*, rituals and sacrifice, and this is true in the external and gross sense, so ably and with great industry and diligence worked out and brought forth in the great commentary of Sayana. Leaving aside the question of discrepancies and quite often the incongruous and poverty-stricken thought that run through this commentary on a large body of the hymns—and after all this is a matter of detail—Sayana's work is consistent in giving us the external and ritualistic meaning of the hymns. And this is a great asset for us, for those who attempt to get into the inner secret through the outer garb that is provided in this monumental work of extraordinary grossness and crudities often bordering on incoherences; it provokes our thought and invites our attention to seek for the secret behind the apparent. But though Sayana gives us the outer and apparent meanings of Riks, though the Gods are treated as Nature-powers, though very often his interpretation with the occasional help of Yaska lends support to the Naturalistic interpretation of modern scholarship, he does not reject, as Sri Aurobindo points out, the spiritual authority of the Veda or 'deny that there is a higher truth concealed in the Riks.' Nor does he affirm that the Vedic hymns are sacrificial compositions of priests, even though his interpretation constitutes a colossal support for ritualism.

But it may be asked: is it a baseless assumption on the part of scholars that the hymns are compositions of the priests for use in the sacrifices? Such a doubt naturally arises in the absence of a correct understanding of the position of the priest in the Vedic society, as well as the real character of the hymns used and chanted in the public sacrifices. For it is the *seer*, Rishi, who was the priest officiating at the ceremonies and the Riks were used for the rituals. The seers were certainly singers and their chants were sung at public sacrifices referring 'constantly to the customary ritual and seem to call for the outward object of these ceremonies, wealth, prosperity, victory over enemies.' While the Riks in their inner sense are profoundly spiritual and the exoteric sense was a mask which alone was perceptible to the outward mind, it was not and need not be merely a mask. Again as the Master points out, they were 'words of power, powerful not only for internal but external things.' The ancient mystics were concerned first and foremost with things of the Spirit, but they were also possessed of Knowledge of occult truths and 'believed that by inner means outer as well as inner results could be produced, that thought and words could be so used as to bring about realisations of every kind, both the human and the divine' *daivam mānusham.*

But a question may arise. How can we say that the seer of profound spiritual knowledge was also the priest for public worship? Of course in the Puranic legends many Rishis are mentioned as priests, *purohits*, and some of them are Rig Vedic names of renown, Vasishtha for example. Is it safe to build and base such a theory on later stories? This difficulty vanishes, once we study the hymns closely, note the tradition in regard to their outer applications also and take the help of the Brahmanas in the context in spite of their obscure symbolism. When we scrutinise, we find not only that the Rishi officiated as the Purohit at the Yajna, but also that the Riks he used are deliberately ritualistic to outward appearance mentioning the implements, external objects, and other things used in the sacrifice, as symbols covering an inner secret known to the Rishi and the initiates. I propose to illustrate this point by citing the example of a well-known Seer who consented to officiate at a Soma sacrifice without the customary goat-immolation. This ritual is entitled *Anjah-Sava* which, Sayana explains, means a rapid direct straight-way offering of libation without the admixture of the sacrificial animal, *anjasā rijunā mārgena ishti-pashu sānkaryam antarena.* The seer-priest is the renowned Shunah-shepa and the hymn for the Anjah-sava is the fifth of the seven Hymns ascribed to him in the First Mandala of the Rik Samnita. It is 1.28, containing nine Riks in which external things like the pressing stones for the extraction of the Soma juice, the platters to receive the juice, the pestle and the mortar, the wooden vessel and other outer things are so plainly mentioned that on the face of it one can conclude that it is a sacrificial composition. When we consider the ideas expressly stated, it is rather childish, devoid of any deep thought, or significance. But when we look deeper into it and ponder over the terms used and the application of the whole hymn in the ritual as explained in the

Brahmanas and also take into account the interesting explanation given by the Brahmanas for certain terms used according to themselves as symbolism, we find ourselves no longer studying the babblings of primitive people deceiving themselves and deceived by an avaricious and cunning priestcraft, but enter into the mysteries of the profound Vedic Yoga of which the seer in question was a notable votary and indeed he embodies one of the types of spiritual victories recorded in the Rig Veda that crowned the toil and ascension of the Aryan soul.

Sayana in his commentary on the 28th hymn of the First Mandala refers to Anjah-Sava as the title of the rapid rite of Soma libation *seen* by the Rishi Shunahshepa in response to the request of other sages and priests that the former must officiate on that day, the day of sacramental bath that is the close of the ceremony. Here mention is made of Aitareya Brahmana 33-5 which narrates the story in brief. The point to be noted in this connection is this that Shunahshepa was unanimously chosen to officiate because he was recognised as one who was the recipient of the grace of the Gods, *devata-anugraha-sampanna*, whose favours helped him to get released from the bonds to which reference for the first time is made in 1.24.

And these bonds are not fastenings with ropes on three parts of the body—the head and the waist and the feet—in spite of the later stories. There is nothing in the 24th hymn, in the text itself to support the extra-ordinarily gross meaning read into the hymn to the effect that he was sold to be immolated in a sacrifice. The legend started slowly with the Aitareya Brahmana in a moderate form, but assumed huge proportions in the Puranas. But a close reading of the hymn itself shows beyond a shadow of doubt that these fastenings refer to the upper, the lower and the middle regions; *uttama*, *adhama*, *madhyama* are the words used in the Rik. And certainly they point to the parts of the being; the upper is the knowledge part represented by the mind and spirit, the lower the material basis, the physical, while the middle refers to the link between Matter and mind, the vital nexus

—the life-principle. The profound sense of the whole hymn reveals the spiritual significance of every line and word in the Riks of that entire hymn. It is not our purpose here to take up the question of Shunahshepa and explain the meaning of the hymn around which so much crust has collected. That has been done elsewhere. It is sufficient to note here that such was the seer whom the priests honoured to officiate at the ceremony.

The Rishi readily consented to conduct the rite and *saw*, 'dadarsha', the method of a rapid rite for the straightway offering of the Soma libation. And the 28th hymn of nine Riks is used for the ritual. We shall first give a close rendering of the Riks which are apparently meant for the rite and make mention of the materials connected with the ceremony and then show how these very things are used as symbols for the inner sacrifice and signify subtle and deep truths pertaining to the Vedic Yoga. And in unveiling the symbols we shall as a matter of course take into account ancient authorities who looked upon these materials as symbols, though not exactly in the way we do, but still were familiar with a general knowledge of symbolism.

Of the nine Riks, in the first four Indra is invoked to come down and drink the Soma; the next four relate to the extraction of the Soma juice and the part of the pestle and mortar, while the last refers to the wooden vessel in which the Soma juice is poured and preserved and the cow-hide in which the dregs are kept.

Here is the English rendering of the hymn, verse by verse.

1. There where the broad-based Stone is high above to press (the Soma juice out), O Indra, drink with eagerness the pourings of the mortar.[1]

Note. *Yatra* 'where' means 'in the ritual', in this action; it can be applied to the outer rite as well as the inner Yaga. Sayana takes the preposition *ava* in the second half to mean

[1] यत्र ग्रावा पृथुबुध्न ऊर्ध्वो भवति सोतवे ।
उलूखलसुतानामवेद्विन्द्र जल्गुलः ॥१॥

avagatya, recognise. This is unwarranted even for the exoteric meaning. The sense of the Rik is this: Indra is above, he is called upon to come *down*, *ava*, to drink *jalgulah* the drippings of the Soma juice from the mortar. In the ritualistic interpretation, *grāva*, stone is taken to be the pestle. Now there is a discrepancy. It is clearly the pressing stone and not pestle. The scholiast calls it pestle because there is the mortar, *ulukhala* in the second line. Pestle and mortar are of wood and used in the Vedic rites to separate the chaff from the grain, they are not used to extract the Soma juice. *Grāva* is stone used to crush the Soma creeper, so that it becomes soft and pressed, yields the juice which is received in the platters. Here in the very first Rik of the hymn the seer significantly refers to the 'stone above' *urdhva*; he does not say it is raised, though for the external rite it can be so interpreted. This stone which is above is Indra's weapon, the *vajra*. Indra is above, his weapon is above; by the blow dealt by the *vajra* even as Vritra, the darkened cloud of adverse forces and ignorance and inertia vanishes, so also the hard matter of body loses its hardness, becomes plastic, free from *tamas*, inertia and its brood of adverse conditions and forces that oppose the release of Rasa, the delight of all experiences to be offered to the Gods, the Cosmic powers of the Godhead. Here the *mortar* is the material body, and it must be noted that earth and every product of it such as the tree, and anything made of wood is symbolic of the physical body and even life and mind as products of the body are very often treated symbolically as of earth and earthern material; of this again later on. This then is the gist of the first Rik. Here this body symbolised by the mortar, 'ulukhala', has yielded the Soma, the *rasa*, its sap, the essence and essential delight for the acceptance of Indra, the Divine mind, the God of the luminous mind, the higher consciousness in the pure mind of heaven, the ruler of this triple world of Matter, Life and Mind. The Rishi addresses Indra invoking his presence to come down and drink the Rasa whose extraction was possible because of the benign blows of the *grava*, the Vajra weapon of Indra himself. Note that this stone is the Vajra weapon, not the gross thunderbolt which is meaningless in the inner sacrifice, but the Vak, the Word wide-based in the Vast above, *urdhva-budhna, prithu-budhna*, as can be gathered from repeated reference to it as such in many lines of the hymns of the Rig Veda, and so explained in the Brahmanas in their moods of symbolic interpretation of the Vedic rituals and Vedic mantras. This Vak, the Word or speech whose source is the Vast above is really that of the luminous mind of heaven, of the higher consciousness and when it functions, its vibrations rush forth and blow off the din and dust of the lower triple body of mind, life and matter, it illumines the mind, energises the life-force, drives out the inertia from the physical body and softens it so that it releases the *rasa* of all the experiences it earned through the life and heart and mind. This, then, is the real character and function of the *grāva* that it is the Word of power issuing forth from the higher consciousness which is the domain of Indra, pregnant with the light of knowledge, but dynamic in its vibrant movement that removes all kinds of coverings and effects with the blow it deals out to the being of the worshipper, *yajamana*, the release of the essence of all delight lying latent and hidden in the vessel, *adhar*, of the human being which is indicated by the symbol of the wooden mortar, *ulukhala.*

2. There where the two platters (to hold the juice), like broad-hips, are laid, O Indra, drink with eagerness the effusions of the mortar.[1]

Now in the external rite of Soma extraction pressing stones are used to crush the creeper, squeeze and make it soft and release the sap. This extraction is called *abhishava.* But the juice is received in two platters, called '*adhi-shavana phalaka*'. They are two shallow dishes, one to receive and and the other to cover. They are broad and likened to broad

[1] यत्र द्वाविव जघनाऽधिषवण्या कृता।
उलूखलसुतानामवेद्विन्द्र जल्गुलः ॥२॥

hips to denote that they are broad and always two, never one without the other.

In the inner sacrifice, these two platters are symbols of Earth and Heaven according to Brahmanic symbology in which case they are the lower physical consciousness and the higher consciousness of the luminous mind. But we do not follow the Brahmanas in unveiling the symbols as they are very often at variance with the many alternatives they themselves suggest or with other Brahmanic interpretations with the result that they become obscure to us. But they shed light on the truth that the stone, platters, mortar, wooden cup or pot, *chamasa* and *kalasha* are all symbolic and should not be taken in their literal sense as unthinking priestcraft would do. The two platters are the mind and life in the body which represent the principles of knowledge and activity. These two are together engaged in receiving the *rasa* yielded by the mortar of the material body and are conjointly there to receive and preserve the juice, the substantial element in all experience for offering to the Gods. In fact it is the twin aspect of knowledge and action, mind and life quite in accord and proper adjustment that makes it possible to receive and preserve the extracted *rasa* which is their common aim and true function. This is in brief the inner meaning of the second verse. It must be noted here that the implements used in the ritual are all mentioned here one by one, at the same time used as symbols which are avowedly said to be symbols, as has been pointed out, and not our invention or the result of ingenious speculation. Now let us pass on to the third Rik.

3. Where (in the rite) the woman learns (or practises) the egress and ingress, O, Indra, drink with eagerness the effusions of the mortar.[1]

This is an interesting Rik. The woman goes out of and comes into the sacrificial hall. The woman is the sacrificer's wife. This is

[1] यत्र नार्यपच्यवमुपच्यवं च शिक्षते ।
उलूखलसुतानामवेद्विन्द्र जल्गुलः ॥३॥

Sayana's explanation of the terms, *nari*, *apachyava* and *upachyava*. The point to be noted here is that no Vedic rite could be performed by any one without a wife. The idea is that the woman, as the Shakti of man, shares the act and its fruit with him whose Shakti she is. I have given egress and ingress as the English equivalents of *apachyava* and *upachyava*; it is not quite accurate and may even mislead, but it has the advantage of leaning more towards the ritualistic interpretation which is best represented in Sayana's commentary. There are other commentators, for instance, Skandaswami, giving a very ludicrous and vulgar meaning which does not merit notice here. Some modern scholars think that it is *rise* and *fall* of the pestle that the woman, the sacrificer's wife marks and learns. But there is no actual mention of pestle at all as has been shown already. In this verse also the words used are significant pointing definitely to the true and inner meaning.

As the action of the Vedic Yoga proceeds, the *rasa* of the whole being of the Yogin the sacrificer, Yajamana, is pressed out and received in the two platters of life and mind in the body and this was stated in the second verse. In the third it is stated that the Shakti of the Purusha, the sacrificer constantly watches and observes and learns the Yogic process in which the higher Force comes down into the being, *upachyava*, and the force from the being goes up or out, *apachyava*, making way for the entry of the higher force into the being. Nari is Nara-Shakti and Nara is either man or God in the Veda denoting one of strength. The power, the Conscious Power of the powerful Soul, *nara*, watches the yogic process of the force of getting in from above and rising up from below, and thus learns, *shikshate*, the secret of the yogic action which is fulfilled in pressing out the juice, the delight of all experiences of the being to be offered to the Higher Powers of the Godhead, the Gods. Thus an intimate knowledge of the secret of the upward and downward movement of the Yoga-force becomes a natural possession under the control of the conscious power of the strong soul that has the strength to give its all to the Gods and receive in return what comes from the Godhead.

4. Where, they fasten the churning staff with a rope as with reins to control (a horse), O, Indra, drink with eagerness the effusions of the mortar.[1]

In the external rite of Soma extraction when the juice is pressed out, it is mixed with milk or curds or corn, *yava*. They are called the three infusions, *gavāshira*, *dadhyāshira* and *yavāshira* respectively. When the Soma juice is to be mixed with this infusion, it is churned; the churning stick is moved by a rope placed round the handle and round a post planted in the ground as a pivot. When the ends of the rope are drawn backwards and forwards, it gives the stick a rotatory motion and the component parts are separated. Thus they tie the churning stick with cords for churning and steadying the vessel, just as with reins one restrains a horse.

[1] यत्र मन्थां विबध्नते रश्मीन्यमितवा इव।
उलूखलसुतानामवेद्विन्द्र जल्गुलः ॥४॥

In the inner sacrifice, from the play of the Yoga-force of knowledge and action through the concord of mind and life, the *rasa,* the flow of delight that is pressed out has to be retained in the body-vessel and not spilt; and for this purpose, the body must be made firm and strong and steady and this object is achieved by the spinal column, made steady charged with the vibrations of the higher consciousness brought by the favours and workings of the Higher Powers. Thus in the first four verses, the pressing out of Soma in the Yajamana's being and the instruments used in the process are mentioned, and the Rishi calls upon Indra to come down and accept the offering of Soma that has been extracted with so much skill and toil and devotion.

The next four Riks are used in the act of straining the Soma juice received in the platters.

5. O, Mortar, if in truth thou art set in every house, here, give forth thy resplendent sound, like the victor's drum.[1]

[1] यच्चिद्धि त्वं गृहेगृह उलूखलक युज्यसे ।
इह द्युमत्तमं वद जयतामिव दुन्दुभिः ॥५॥

Here is a pronounced difficulty in the gross sense. Now, the mortar is addressed and called upon to give a loud sound like the drum of the conquerors. Mortar never makes noise without the rapid rise and fall of the pestle which is nowhere mentioned in the whole hymn though *grāva* in the first verse is pressed to yield that meaning in the ritualistic interpretation as it has to be somehow managed. Now in the inner interpretation, the idea is quite clear. Mortar is of course the physical being. In every house, in every man, there is a mortar, there is a material body but every body does not shed the precious juice. But, the Rishi says, you are splendid and have given out the essence of all the experiences for offering even though you are *jada* matter, thick with inertia and darkness. You have trained yourself to respond to the touches and influence of the higher Powers that are invoked by the Yajamana and have yielded the *rasa* of your being. Therefore you can loudly proclaim your victory over the tamasic forces that oppose the release of the *rasa*. Hence like the drum of the conqueror you can proclaim; it is not every mortar, the material body of every one, that is so successful as you.

6. O Lord of the Forest, the wind blows fast in front of thee, O Mortar, for Indra that he may drink, press forth the Soma juice.[1]

Vanaspati, literally lord of the forest is used to indicate any tree or plant or part and product of the forest. Mortar being made of wood is addressed here Vanaspati. The mortar is called upon to press out the juice, and the wind blows fiercely, *vivāti*! How does the wind blowing fast or fiercely help the mortar to yield the juice? Sayana says the wind blows fast in front of the mortar because of the speed of the pestle's constant blow! Where is the pestle in the Rik? Here again, the Rik is seemingly ritualistic, but really reveals secrets of the action of Yoga-force in the inner sacrifice. Mortar is indeed the material body; Vayu is the life-force which is stimulated and by

[1] उत स्म ते वनस्पते वातो विवात्यग्रमित् ।
अथो इन्द्राय पातवे सुनु सोममुलूखल ॥६॥

far strengthened at this stage, thus helping the body to give out the *rasa*. Without a strong life-force awake and active nothing can be done in the body whatever may be the light of knowledge that may fall upon it; the light does not enter a feeble frame, and even if it enters the weak material cannot hold it without a strong vital support. Only when it is endowed with a strong and well-poised life-force in action, can the body be willing to give itself joyfully i.e., the *rasa* for Indra's drink.

7. Implements of sacrifice, best of strength-givers, sport high on like the two bay-horses of Indra munching noisily.[1]

Here again, the dual number is used in the address. Who are addressed is left to be understood and in the ritualist's interpretation, they are the inevitable pestle and mortar and they give food, *vāja*. They are the implements of sacrifice *āyaji*. Because of the

[1] आयजी वाजसातमा ता ह्युच्चा विजर्भृतः ।
हरी इवान्धांसि बप्सता ॥७॥

movement of the pestle in the mortar, they give loud sound; *uchcha* is thus interpreted without warrant. The straight meaning is *uchchaih vihāra*; they sport high on like the two horses of Indra champing grain.

In the esoteric interpretation, the implements are really the two platters; they are of the forest, *vanaspati*, as the next verse confirms by stating so expressly. They are the procurers of strength in its plenitude, *vājasātamam*. They sport high above, like Indra's horses. Because of their conjoint action and movement in the upper regions of the being of the Yogin, the Yajamana, they procure strength increasingly and receive the *rasa* of the being for offering. Indra's two horses are used as a simile here for their capacity for enjoyment. It is much more than a simile. Life and mind themselves representing force of action and light of knowledge are the twin vehicles of the Divine Mind, the ruler of the triple words and king of the Gods, Indra.

8. O, Lords of the forest, mighty with the mighty pressors, press out today the most

sweet Soma juice for Indra's drink.[1]

Rishwa means great or mighty; to press out the juice strength is necessary; hence with the help of other priests present in the sacrifice the juice is to be pressed out of the platters.

But in the inner ritual, the Rishi calls upon the platters of Life and Mind to press out the Rasa with the help of the mighty Powers of Knowledge and Power who are ever ready to render assistance to the aspiring soul that has consecrated itself for the Godward life; and this demands the giving up of all one is and has for the acceptance and enjoyment of the higher Powers of the Universal Purusha to whom all that one is and has really belongs.

9. What remains, hold in the two chamasa vessels, pour the Soma on the filter and set the residue on the cow-hide.[2]

[1] ता नो अद्य वनस्पती ऋष्वावृष्वेभिः सोतृभिः।
इन्द्राय मधुमत्सुतम् ॥८॥

[2] उच्छिष्टं चम्वोर्भर सोमं पवित्र आ सृज।
नि धेहि गोरधि त्वचि ॥९॥

In the ritual we know the juice is purified and strained and then poured into a large wooden cup or vessel called the *drona-kalasha.* The dregs are set in the cow-hide.

Thus the outer rite was rapidly performed straightway offering the beverage to Indra who is invoked to come down to drink in the first four Riks.

In the inner sacrifice, when we take into consideration the context, the *chamu* or the *chamasa* is a bowl and the two bowls are nothing else but the cups of the vital body and the mental body which were referred to by the symbolic *platters,* when they were used for the extraction of the *rasa.* But now, when the process is complete they are referred to as separate vessels to signify the yogic secret that though life and mind function in the body as part of it, they really are separate entities and are separated by the Yoga-force for readjustment in the new set-up for the consummation of the Yoga. Those who have studied Sri Aurobindo on the Ribhus can not fail to appreciate the Yogic fact that out of the one bowl, four bowls are made for the

Yogin by the Ribhus, who were once human beings, but have become gods by dint of their *tapasya* and help Indra in a variety of ways; they are indeed 'artisans of Immortality'. Thus the juice of delight is taken up in the two bowls of Life and Mind. They are then poured into the Kalasha which is the material body. The residue is kept in the hide of cow which is the covering and protection of the Ray of Light in the physical frame of man.

* * *

We have stated that symbolism is the key to unlock the secret of the Veda; but the device of symbolism dating back from the age of the Rig Veda has been used in the latter scriptures also, closing with the Epics, Puranas and Tantric works. But it is the Brahmanas following the Vedas that openly gave symbolic explanations of the rituals and necessarily of the hymns used in them and this fact was recognised by later authors in their commentaries on the Brahmanas and on the Upanishads which form parts of them. The Brihadaranyaka Upanishad forms the close of the 14th chapter of the Shatapatha Brahmana. Out of a number of examples we shall choose one to show how symbols were interpreted by Acharyas like Shankara, though that does not mean they recognised the close-knit symbolism of the hymns of the Rig Veda rich with deep meaning and profound truths of spiritual wisdom. But it undoubtedly shows that these later teachers of Vedanta know that there are many passages in the Upanishads and the Veda Samhitas which are symbolic, while some others are riddles and puzzles and the like. The passage occurs in Br. Up. 2.2.3. It refers to a bowl *chamasa* with its base or bottom above and opening below. 'The Glory that is the universe of forms or the All-form is laid in it', says the text.[1] The Upanishad, rather the Brahmana itself proceeds to give the explanation on which Shankara remarks: 'What is this *chamasa* with hole below and base above? It is the head which is above like a chamasa bowl,

[1] अर्वाग्बिलः चमस ऊर्ध्वबुध्नः तस्मिन् यशो निहितं विश्वरूपम्।

and the mouth is the aperture below. In that bowl is laid the All-form. Just as Soma is kept in the bowl, the universe of forms or the All-form is set in the head etc.'[1] This is just an instance to show that the symbolic meaning was recognised and quoted by philosophers of later times even though they were immured with the idea and spirit of their age when the tradition that the Veda was a book for rituals, *karmakanda*, had long firmly settled itself in the minds of scholars and leaders of thought with great repute for originality. We may note in passing that when a meaning is not directly conveyed by the word, when it is not evident, but indirect and concealed, it is called *paroksha-vachana* which term is used in the Brahmana-Upanishads whenever there is symbolism or riddle or something apparently incongruous or even

[1] कः पुनरसाववार्ग्बिलश्चमस ऊर्ध्वबुध्नः ? इदं तत्; शिरः चमसाकारं हि तत्; कथम् ? एवं हि अर्वाग्बिलः मुखस्य बिलरूपत्वात्, शिरसो बुध्नाकारत्वात् ऊर्ध्वबुध्नः। तस्मिन् यशो निहितं विश्वरूपमिति—यथा सोमः चमसे, एवं तस्मिन् शिरसि विश्वरूपं नानारूपं निहितं स्थितं भवति .....

repulsive. When we meet with such passages, it is a sure indication that the sense is concealed and that it is a hint to find out the secret behind the apparent language.

Now in unveiling the symbols of the Riks used in the rapid rite of Soma, we have taken the help of other passages of the Rig Veda and taken into account the Yajurveda, the Veda most important for the ritualist as well as some Brahmana passages that have bearing on the question. We have already spoken of the two platters—*adhishavaniya*—as symbolic and explained it in a way that fits in with the rest of the symbols in the rite. And the White Yajurveda and the Shatapatha Brahmana (2.9.4.) proclaim them to be so, stating that the two platters are symbols of Earth and Heaven. With reference to *grāva* this Brahmana says it is *vajra* and the blow it gives destroys what it calls *pāpma*, evil (or sin), the dark and opposing block of forces that prevents the release of the juice of delight, the flow of Soma; it is not the Soma that is destroyed, but the *papma*, *papma hatah, na somah.* The *grāva* is above, its base is broad, the Vast above; it is the weapon of Indra who is above, it is Vajra in the outer world, but its character in the inner sense is Vak, speech, the Word from the higher heights coming from the region of the Indra. This is clear from many passages of the Rig Veda. The Gods are above and Indra is certainly above, he is invoked to come down to man and to accept his offering. He is there above, and lifts us, mortals that we may live above. We shall cite a few passages here:

1. O, Indra of hundred activities, stay on above for our growth (or protection) in this our toil for plenitude....(I.30.6.)

2. Stay on above like the God Savitr for our growth (or protection); Thou, above, bestower of plenitude....(I.36.13).

3. Thou above, guard us from evil, with thy flame of Intuitive vision burn every devouring demon....(I.36.14).

Urdhva-budhna, *uru-budhna*, *prithu-budhna* are in frequent use in the hymns e.g. IV.2.5; I.169.6; X.47.3. This *budhna* is the base or foundation which is said to be above, *urdhva*, extensive and vast, *uru*, broad and wide, expansive, *prithu*. It is used as an adjective to *grava* and to some other things that are to come from above, related to the Gods. In a verse Indra is called upon to bestow upon the Rishi the wealth which is at once deep, *gabhira*, wide and vast, *uru*, based in the vast, *prithu-budhna*. It is an interesting Rik which reveals the real nature of the wealth above for which the Rishis prayed and toiled. "Riches,—full of powerful Mantras (*su-brahmanam*) God-possessing, high above, wide and based on vast foundations above, virile with the Rishi's inspiration, conquering the enemy (that is the opposing force) —such riches, mighty and colourful, vouchsafe to us" (X.47.3). Similar is the Stone, Indra's *grava* of the lofty heights. It is the Heaven's bolt of thunder which is indeed a symbol of the voice of Indra above which is invoked to drop down for the destruction of the enemy (II.30.5). The 'Stone' voices with the sound of the singer's chant (I.83.6). The 'Stone' attracts with its voice the mind of Indra (I.84.3). "Go you both (Indra and Vayu) there where the stone voices forth"

(I.135.17). Again, the stones of the lofty heights (III.53.12), 'the voiceful stone laid on the altar' (V. 31.4), a variegated stone set in the midst of Heaven (V.47.3). These 'stones' are of Heaven and from the heights of being; they are not of earth, not the common stones used to press the creeper Soma. For the Soma is of Heaven and pressed by the symbolic stones for offering to the Gods, *tam twam devebhyo gravabhih sutah* (IX.80.4), 'pressed by the Stone, O, Soma, you enter the sieve strainer bestowing valiant strength on the chanter' (IX.67.19). These are a few lines out of the hundreds one frequently comes across in the hymns that go to show that the 'Stone' and other objects used in the ritual are symbolic and reveal the inner truths of the Vedic Yoga of which the *seers* were adepts. We shall close this short study with one last reference to a Rik in Vamadeva's hymns (IV.27.5) where the *kalasha* though outwardly a beaker, refers certainly to the body. It is a famous hymn quoted in the Upanishads and as such is admittedly, even according to the ritualistic commentaries, rich with spiritual truths and therefore of inner significance.

'Let Indra accept the white beaker, annointed with the cow's yield, filled with the luminous liquid etc.' Here the beaker, *kalasha*, is the *drona-kalasha* used in the rite. But it is symbolic and indicates the body which is annointed with the Ray of Light, it is 'white' i.e. it is pure and filled with the shining *rasa*, the liquid of Soma, Delight. Here is a fine specimen of a hymn which openly proclaims the spiritual truth of Vamadeva in the womb for Divine birth and his experience in the iron-gated cities etc; it uses plainly, in the last verse quoted above, ritualistic objects. This would be incongruous in the extreme, if something deeper were not meant, deeper than the beaker and milk and the juice of a creeper.

Such is the character of the Vedic ritual meant for outward worship; such is the nature of the symbolic objects prayed for and the materials used in the sacrificial rite; such also is the nature of the deeper truths of the hymns which keep to the inner sense quite closely and yet maintain to a large extent the outward form and meaning suitable to the understanding and use of the un-initiate. The salient feature that must be noted is this that while the hymns occasionally throw the exoteric sense overboard when so warranted by a necessity for the esoteric pressing overtly for prominence, still in most hymns the outer meaning leaps to the eye and the hymn 1.28 used in the rite of Anjah-sava is a typical example to show that the ritual is no ordinary rite and that the hymn is not an off-hand or laboured composition of the priestcraft, that it has a revelatory significance and meaning deeper than what strikes the mind at first thought. And Shunah-shepa is a seer of renown, a seer whose victorious release from the triple bond of mind and life and body has given rise to allegories and impossible legends, whose other hymns, and many Riks in them, rank high among the plainly spiritual passages of lofty ideas and occult truths in the hymnal text. Thus when we study the hymns with the necessary background the secret of the Veda becomes apparent, the inner truth becomes lucid and transparent and we begin to appreciate more fully and intelligently the Master's words that the Vedic Seer was also a priest who officiated at public sacrifices and chanted the hymns whose real purport, the inner truth of Divine Wisdom was known to him and the initiate.

SECTION TWO

SIDELIGHTS ON TANTRA

In this brief study we shall make an attempt to appreciate the basic principles that underlie the Agamas, generally called Tantra Shastra. We shall make a general reference to their relation to the Vedic and Vedantic schools of philosophic thought and spiritual discipline. We shall take note of the salient features and evaluate, in the light of Sri Aurobindo's teachings, the part they have played in the past which has trickled down to the current times. When we look upon the past of India, upon the lines of her cultural history in its meandering course, with all the vicissitudes of such a long life that has few parallels elsewhere, we are struck by a consistent note. It is a note that permeates every successive attempt to revive the ancient spirit and restate in the language and form suited to the conditions of the age the high ideals, the subtle ideas and sublime truths perceived and worked out by the early builders of Indian society in its infancy as well as in adolescence. What is this perpetual note that arrests our attention? Certainly, it is the presence of a large synthesis conceived and worked out first by the ancient architects of society, the seers and sages of the Vedic Age and later in its decline taken up by the revivalist attempts of the Brahmanas and the Upanishads. Nowhere this spirit and vision of synthesis is so open and exacting as in the teachings of the Gita which heals up the hiatus or the apparent gulf of the intermediate ages and builds a comprehensive system having for its basis the spirit of the Veda and the substance of the Vedanta, takes up all the accumulated knowledge of the past, assimilates the essentials into the body and spirit of its instructions, and presents a really grand synthesis not as a metaphysical system but as a comprehensive teaching for application under all conditions of life.

But there has been all along another distinctive Synthesis embodied in the teachings of Agamas which, while professing general allegiance to the Vedic systems of philosophy and thought and spiritual discipline, is apparently different in its method of approach and is comprehensive, all-inclusive in its spirit, devoid of the exclusiveness associated with all the religious schools and rituals based upon the Smritis and Shrutis of Vedic ceremonialism. It is difficult to plumb exactly into their origins, much less to find the precise period of the beginnings of their teachings though the extant works of the Agamas can be traced to approximate periods of India's history. For we must note that the substance of the teachings may have and certainly has come from early ages, though the written texts may have appeared later on at different times which may be ascertained with less difficulty. Let us first be sure of the sense in which the term Agama is used and came to be called Tantra and then proceed with the main principles of the framework of the Agamas in general and the Shakta Tantras in particular.

In dealing with the purposes of the study of *Vyākarana*, Sanskrit Grammar, Patanjali uses the word Agama in the sense of Veda or Vedic knowledge; and in the Yoga Sutras he speaks of three criteria of knowledge—Perception (pratyaksha), Inference (anumana), and Revelation or authentic utterance (agama). Thus we find that because all sacred scriptures were considered to be revealed the Veda was termed Agama; and when another class of literature, viz. Tantra, scriptural in import, appeared and began to hold sway over a vast mass of people, the term Nigama was applied to Veda while Agama though not exclusively but generally came to denote Tantra on the one hand and ensure its sanctity like the Veda on the other. Now it is well known that the Rishis of the Veda are not authors of the Veda but seers of the Mantra while the Veda is understood to be eternal even as the Divine Wisdom that is embodied in it. The Agamas, whoever may be their writers and whatever their dates be, are held to be essentially Scriptures revealed by the Supreme Shiva or Hari according to the nature and class of the Agamas concerned.[1] Let us leave

[1] The dates of the extant Agamas even when they are settled with certainty do not at all mean that the teachings they embody came

aside for consideration the Bauddha and Jaina Agamas which openly disclaim any Vedic authority and purport in fact to oppose and supplant the ancient tradition, and we have the Vaishnava, the Shaiva and the Shakta

---

to birth along with the books. It is necessary to strike a note of caution on this point in view of the current beliefs among a section of the educated classes, Indian and Western, that the Agamas were later inventions or scriptural adjustments wrought by the endeavours of later writers. Shiva-worship side by side with the Vishnu-worship was current in the Southern (Tamil) India as early as the first and second century of the Christian Era as is evidenced in the sacred poems of Nayanmars, Shaiva Saints, and the Prabandhams of Alwars, Vaishnava Saints, whose times extend from the 2nd to the 8th century. Not only worship, but references to Agamas are frequent therein. In the North, the Besnagar Pillar Inscription of the 2nd century B.C. bears clear testimony to Vishnu worship in temples. The Inscription records the erection of Garuda Pillar in the temple of Vasudeva and indicates thereby that that worship had been accepted by a foreign Greek ambassador from Taxila.

That the major Puranas and the main Agamas of Shaiva and Vaishnava persuasion were written and completed by the end of the Gupta period is admitted on all hands by students of history. But Vasudeva worship is referred to by Panini whose time is at least some four centuries before Christ. Thus it is wrong to deduce from the available texts that the teachings themselves started with these books. It is quite possible that Shiva worship was a feature of the Indus Valley Civilisation and the recent researches based upon the excavations throw some light on prehistoric India and have given shock to the accepted notions of historians in regard to stories of Ancient India.

Agamas. The Vaishnava Agamas look upon Vishnu as the Supreme and other gods and goddesses his aides; so do the Shaiva Agamas assign the highest position to Shiva. The Shakta Agamas too claim the most superior position for the Goddess in practice.[1] But in theory She is not put above Vishnu or Shiva. She is indeed the Creatrix of the Trinity, Brahma, Vishnu and Rudra---the Mother of the Universe. But She is also acclaimed as the Yoga-Maya of Vishnu as in Chandi Saptashati or as in other texts the Para Shakti, the Supreme Consort of Shiva. There is another notable difference between the Shakta and the other two classes of Agamas. For while the Shaiva and Vaishnava Agamas continue and preserve the Vedic tradition of confining their knowledge and application only to the four Varnas with

[1] We must note that this was a radical departure from the Vedantic tradition. For while the tradition looked upon the Purusha as the Lord of all and the One Substratum of All, the Shakta Agama i.e. Tantra increasingly looked to the Energy aspect of the Supreme, to the Prakriti in effect and this departure was responsible, as pointed out by Sri Aurobindo, for the later loss of its purity of intention in the mechanism of its means.

some restraint, the Shakta declares in a more liberal spirit that it is for all people irrespective of their Varna. It is the scripture of the common man. All the Agamas are also known as the Tantra Shastra. Tantra in Sanskrit has many meanings; but the one significance of relevance to us here is *act*. Act—and ritual is an act—is the one characteristic common to all the Agamas and hence they have come to be known as the Tantra Shastra.

A striking feature common to these Agamas is the high reverence in which they hold the Vedas. They do not, as is imagined by many, run counter to the spirit of the Veda. On the contrary, they declare that the knowledge in the Veda is high, beyond the reach of common men and claim to hold in themselves the substance and essence of the supreme knowledge embedded in that Scripture. And indeed it is so. For while the Upanishads represent the revivalist attempts for the recovery of the Jnana portions of the Vedas, the practical side of the Vedic teaching, not as related to the Ritual—for that was the care of the Brahmanas—but as concerning the inner life of the seeker, the esoteric teaching as we would put it, was sought to be revived, continued and preserved by these later Yogas and Tantras. As Sri Aurobindo observes: "....The mental images of the Vedic gods figured in the mantras (were replaced) by mental forms of the two great deities, Vishnu and Shiva, and their Shaktis and by corresponding physical images which are made the basis both for external worship and for the Mantras of inward adoration and meditation, while the psychic and spiritual experience which the inner sense of the Vedic hymns expresses finally disappeared into the psycho-spiritual experience of Puranic and Tantric religion and Yoga." Such knowledge as this—of the building of the inner life—was traditionally handed down from father to son, from Guru to Shishya and the Agamas represent a worthy compilation and preservation of this inheritance from the forefathers. There are many traces of the Vedic influence and outlook in these Agamas. There is, for instance, a monotheism in them. It is now Shiva, now Vishnu or Hari who is the Supreme. There is also, as in the Rig Veda, an apparent polytheism. For many are the deities worshipped and invoked by the aspirant—though their position is one of subordination to, and ultimately identity with the Supreme. There is even a tendency to Monism perceptible in the Shakta scriptures. The devotee worships the Deity and finds his glorious culmination in the final act of complete identification and merging in the Higher—eliminating all difference between the worshipper and the worshipped.

But these Agamas are not a mere conglomeration of various systems of teachings and past traditions. They work up a large synthesis instead. And synthesis is no collection or heaping up of diverse elements; it is not eclecticism either. The synthesis we meet with in the Agamas is a living whole in which every element of value is preserved and falls into its just position and proportion—all together making quite a new and developing system which embraces the entire life in its sweep, the man in the individual and man in the aggregate, man the thinker and the doer, man the soul. This synthesis of the Tantra is in fact more comprehensive than the synthesis of the Gita and in a sense more in consonance with the Intention in life. For the ultimate teaching of the Gita comes to this: action is unavoidable, none can subsist without it. So make the best of it, use it—such of it as allows itself to be so used—first of all for your own moral and spiritual elevation leading to a progressive surrender to the Lord of all so that once you are completely given to Him you may have nothing more to do with this transitory and unhappy world, even though you may continue to do work for the sake of others. Life is a lever for rising upwards and shooting beyond it, not a field to be worked upon and cherished as an enjoyable creation of the Divine Being. The Tantric synthesis however looks upon life with a different and other vision. There is nothing to be rejected from what the Supreme Shakti has created. Even that which the Gita enjoins upon all seekers to reject, the *bhoga*, need not be given up. After all the world is for the *bhoga* of the Ishwara or the Ishwari and man at his highest, representing as he does an effective portion of Him or Her, must enjoy the *bhoga*, conscious of his part as the vehicle or centre of the Enjoyer. That this *bhoga-marga*, Vama-marga as it is called, later fell into disrepute and degeneracy is quite another matter which could be easily explained and does not detract from the sublime conception at the base, the high standard of purity and sincerity that was expected of one if he was to discharge conscientiously his responsibility as an unsullied channel of the Joy of *Bhoga*. It means a tremendous labour of discipline and self-exceeding, in one's own personal and inner, and the outer and collective life—a continuous action, *tantra*, on so many planes.

Let us now turn to a closer view of the Tantric system and scrutinise the four famous parts, *pada*--which go to make up the whole. Every way of religious and spiritual life has a basis to stand upon, a metaphysical base providing the philosophical Truths underlying the system, its genesis, rationale, the aim. In fact it is the strength and validity of this source of inspiration that determine the course and power of the outflowing manifestation. A systematised presentation (in intellectual terms) of the underlying Idea, a rational working out of its ways and means of expression, an examination of its fundamentals—in the premisses and in the conclusions—*vis à vis* other prevailing Idea-truths, is what we would call the metaphysical basis of a system and the Tantra Shastra has doubtless a philosophy, a metaphysics of its own. If the esoteric message of the Vedas is the substance of its practical teaching, the Vedanta with the Sankhya in a modified form provides the background, we may say, even the backbone of the philosophy of the Tantra. The Supreme is One and All is He. Only there it is Brahman, here it is Vishnu, Shiva or Shakti. The psychology of the Tantra is the psychology of the Sankhyas which itself is a side-product of the Upanishadic thought. These teachings are developed and extended so as to apply to a larger and larger part of man; the emphasis is sought to be shifted from the soul and mind to the other parts of the being, the heart and emotions and the will as well. In fact it is a restatement of the Wisdom of the Upanishads in terms suited to the changing conditions in which society was passing with varying stresses on the different elements that go to make up the complex personality of man. But this Knowledge-part, *Jnana-pada*, could not be all. At best it can provide a satisfying and even a compelling understanding of the aim and purpose of life. Beyond that it has to go, it has to be accompanied by steps taken to put it into practice, to translate it into action. And the Tantra has the second *pada*, the *Yoga-pada* for the purpose.

It is certainly not that Yoga was born with the Agamas or the Tantriks or that there were no Yogins before they came. It cannot be said either that even Raja Yoga was first propounded by Patanjali. The truth is that Yoga is as old as the Vedas at least and the Institution of Sacrifice, *Yajna*, in the Vedas is just a symbol of the one Yoga in which the Rishis were ceaselessly engaged, the Yoga by which they endeavoured, invoked and received in themselves the gods from high on. In the very nature of things there was no set uniformity in every detail of the individual pursuits of the Yoga though in large outlines they always corresponded. Handed down by tradition for centuries, it was perhaps Patanjali who first picked up one line of Yoga, and methodised the system of Raja Yoga in his famous Sutras. But Tantric Yoga goes beyond that, it infuses an inner discipline on the lines marked out by the Guru to the disciple. Life is sought to be purified, uplifted and equipped for effective embodiment and living the truths in accordance with the principles laid out in the *Jnana-pada*.

The Tantra Shastra does not stop with the individual. It recognises that for all purposes man is but a member of the larger society around. He influences those around and is influenced by their movements, by their thoughts, aspirations and actions to a greater extent than he normally affects the aggregate. It is not enough to educate and develop one unit. It is indispensable to mould the general environment also on the same lines so that there could be an identity of aspiration, a mutually helpful and congenial intercourse between the individual and the collective. It recognises also that human mind in the mass is less attracted to the abstract and the subtle and goes on to provide significant rituals and ceremonies by which it could be gradually drawn to the inner truth of things. This is the *Kriya-pada.* External ceremonies, ritual, worship have played a notable part in the awakening of the naturally extrovert consciousness of man to the reality of an Inner Presence; they impinge upon the senses and sense-faculties of man with considerable force and leave impressions which in the cumulative result effect an opening through some part into the larger being of himself. Effort at such social and collective religious practices is encouraged. Congregational worship has a stimulating effect and power of invocation not generally realised by most. The atmosphere created by the pressure of a single Idea, a single mounting aspiration in a multitude of hearts simultaneously striving for the same end gets charged with a force and intensity which the individuals share, consciously or unconsciously, each benefitting by the all, each individual aspiration and realisation contributing to the general but also absorbing and growing on the strength and nourishment received from the total and the general. It is in this light that the elaborate ritual-cum-worship aspect of the Tantra is to be examined. This aspect of the Tantra bears a close resemblance to and recalls the Ritual of the Brahmanas, the Yajna of the Veda. There is no more the full figure of the Yajna; yet an important ritual in the construction of Temple and the installation of the Idol is the *Kumbha-abhisheka*, considered to be a *Yaga*. Thus even the tradition of the old ritual ceremony is absorbed and carried forward in a newer form.

And this is not all. The seeker is given a philosophy with which he equips himself intellectually; he is initiated into a Yoga that could yield the truth of the philosophy for his living; he is provided with an environment and an outer scaffolding suited to the growth and outflowering of his faith and realisation. But the spiritual effort, fostered and built up with such an all-round care and eye for detail, is not meant to be bottled up in its results within the limits of the individual frame. Liberation of the soul from the bonds of the lower Prakriti and a release into the heights of the Spirit does not form the end of such a comprehensive endeavour. The ideal individual of the Tantric Yoga has a responsibility to others less fortunate than himself, he is looked upon as a *Siddha*, a perfect individual for the outpouring of the Shakti he is in communion with. He has to have dealings with men and society, he has to discharge all the responsibilites that devolve on him by virtue of the pre-eminent position he has attained, not without some help from the society. He has to guide and lead others. The Shastra lays down the code of conduct, the ways of functioning—the *Charya*—for these mentors of men. Relations and activities of men in the spiritual path are governed by rules and modes of conduct other than those that are prescribed by the Dharma of the age for the laity. That is because their thoughts and their actions proceed on a different basis; they have another motive-force and other ends in view. Their attitude to life, their outlook on the world, is different from that of common humanity and things do not appear to them in the same hue and light in which they do to others. As a rule man looks only at the surface of things, thinks—when he does at all—with an insufficient faculty called mind and proceeds as best as he could. But one who has effected a change in his make-up by dint of *tapasya*, and stationed himself on a deeper basis necessarily governs his life-movement with different considerations which may at times strike the convention-ridden mind as opposed to reason or morality even as the actions of an adult human being may well appear to be harsh, cruel and stupid—when they are really otherwise—to an infant. The Tantra Shastra recognises and provides for the need of such a higher type of being to proceed on different basis of action in the fourth *pada*, the *Charya-pada* and enjoins upon him to work out the progressive weal of the rest. Mark the three ways of worship of the Tantriks: the godly way, *divya bhāva*, the way of the hero, *vira bhāva*, and that of the animal, *pashu bhāva*, which alone is governed by the ordinary stereotyped rules of conduct.

This in brief is the rationale of the four padas of the Tantra, the Jnana-pada, Yoga-pada,

Kriya-pada and Charya-pada. A Tantra is whole and complete only when it has these four parts. We can now better appreciate the large spirit that has actuated the Tantric sages. But no human institution fashioned by human hands in Time is known to have escaped the decay and disease inevitable with the wear of age and the Tantric system has been no exception. And we need not be surprised when we find votaries of the Tantra attaching exclusive importance to the externals of the cult, to the minutiae and formulae totally forgetful of the original intention of the system-builders. Thus when it is asserted that what is of utmost importance in the Kriya-pada is strict observance, to the very letter, of the requirements in measurement and design in the construction of the temple and performance of the ritual or when it is sought to enforce uniform rules for all relating to details of daily life as all-sufficing commandments of the Charya-pada, one can only smile if he has enough detachment or sigh at human stupidity which competes with the march of ages in pulling down lofty structures of the ancients.

Before concluding this section on the Tantric synthesis we cannot resist the temptation of drawing attention to the parallel between this and the New Synthesis, the synthesis worked out in the Teachings of Sri Aurobindo. Not that this our system has been modelled after the Tantric, though it is true that the Tantric truths have gone into the making of it even as the Vedantic conceptions have. But they do not, by any means, form the prototypes; they are important elements; we will not go into the question further for the moment but only point out an interesting correspondence between the Tantric-Quartette and the Quartette of writings Sri Aurobindo found necessary to broad-base his vast system, for Metaphysics and Philosophy, for the realisation of the fundamental truths in one's being, for the development of social psychology in consonance with the principles enunciated and finally for the actual working out of the Unity of man.

II

It is not accurate to describe this ancient religion of India now current as Puranic. Neither the Gods of the current religion nor the metaphysics and philosophy—Shastra—are really Puranic in origin. The Puranas are compilations of the legendary lore of the country, giving different accounts of the cosmogony of the universe—accounts of the primary creation, the secondary creation, narrations of the geneology of the progenitors of mankind, cycles of time, rolls of the dynasties of kings, etc.—*purānam pancha-lakshanam*. The Puranas are more historical—if history they can be called—interspersed with philosophical or religious stories for the mental and moral elevation of man and society. The Gods of the Hindu religion are in fact Tantric Gods. And the Gods of the Tantra are not sudden arrivals on the scene. They are really a continuation of the line of Gods of the Veda. Not in the same form and name of course, but with necessary modifications inevitable with the incidence of Time on tradition.

The Vedic Gods, as we have noted elsewhere while dealing with the subject in fuller detail, have a twofold aspect to the seers of the Veda. In their exterior aspect they are essentially Nature-powers. Agni is the elemental fire, Indra the rain-god, Surya the solar body, Maruts the storm-gods and so on. But they have another, psychological character also and this was more important to those initiated into the mystery of the Vedic religion. These Gods are powers indeed, but not merely the powers of Nature. They are rather higher Powers, Personalities of the Godhead having Cosmic field for their action. There are also lower gods who preside over the elemental forces of nature, over movements in the physical world and also movements in the inner world of man. Besides presiding over the Fire element in creation, Agni is looked upon as the deity controlling and promoting the upward flame, the *agni* in man stationed on the various levels of his being—as the *agni* in life, *prana-agni*, as the flame of aspiration in the heart, as the consuming quest for knowledge in the mind.

He has other functions also. Similarly, Indra is the God governing the higher regions of the luminous mind, the Maruts controlling and contributing to the life-forces and thought-powers of man. Thus the Gods are cosmic Powers with specific functions in the external world of Nature as well as with more important and significant charge in the inner world that supports it from behind and above. The sages of the Tantras carried on the tradition in the essentials that mattered. The Gods are very much the same here also, only the external functions in their physical aspect which predominate in the common mind of the early times have been appropriately relegated to the background when they are not altogether dispensed with. Thus Agni of the Veda continues in the Tantra, with a change of name certainly, yet with the same functions and even the new name, Kumara, Child, is significant for the Agni-origin it preserves. Agni is Kumara, Child of the Supreme Shiva. In the Rig Veda Agni is in the forefront of the Gods, their guide, their messenger. Here he is their chief of Powers who leads them to victory, the commander behind whom they line up. In the Veda Agni is regarded by the seers as the all-effecting and all-knowing pilot of their journey. Kumara is also looked up to for his immense store of knowledge and wisdom by these seers of later times. Again, the mighty Indra is there, but in the Tantra and the Puranas his part is taken up by Rudra the powerful who brooks no obstacle. The hosts of Indra—the Maruts—continue as the *pramathas* of Rudra. Indra the *marutwān*, leader of the hosts of Maruts, the storm-gods or life-powers, continues to play his effective part as Rudra the lord of the *pramathas*, Pramathanatha. The Sun, the Highest God of the Veda is also here as Vishnu—a name which is applied to the Supreme Sun in the Rig Veda itself. Aditi the mother of All is not there under the same nomenclature, but there is the Supreme Shakti, called variously Uma, Gouri etc. All the important Gods are there. The other minor gods with mainly physical functions and less of the psychological have been consigned to the position of the *Dik-palakas*, guardians of the several quarters or of some other minor importance. Newer Gods have arrived, true, but the older ones have not been altogether supplanted and totally forgotten, they retain their due supremacy though in different form.

We have referred to that interesting feature of the Tantra, namely the recognition of the Supreme Deity as the Highest with a simultaneous adoration of a number of other deities. The sages of the Tantra do not see any inconsistency in the position, for they recognise that this creation is not a unitary system but a gradation of worlds spread over a rising tier of consciousness and planes and the various Gods and Goddesses are higher beings, powers and entities deriving their authority from the Supreme to take their part, and act or preside over their spheres of domain. There is a regular hierarchy of Gods some of whom are far above the highest heavens of human reach. But there are also Gods and Goddesses closer to the human level. They are more readily accessible to those who aspire to them and in some cases the seeker on the Tantric path looks to the aid and lead of these deities in his effort. They are endowed with capacities and powers beyond normal human possibility, but they are not all for that reason divine in nature. There are higher and lower classes of them, *Uchcha* and *Kshudra* Devatas. Those that are nearest to the earth-plane, swarming in the vital world overtopping the physical, are usually of the latter type. They respond very readily to the approaches of those who seek their help, but they do so mainly for their own purpose, namely to get hold of the particular human vehicle and convert it into a centre for their activity on the earth. They may and do answer the call of the seeker in the beginning but in the end they let him down, rather roughly, once their purpose is fulfilled. The seeker is misled, his inner progress comes to a standstill if it does not end in disaster. The Kshudra-devatas mislead the seeker with petty glamorous gifts, induce a false sense of progress and *siddhi*, prevent the dawn of real Jnana which would expose their whole game and succeed in enslaving the man for their purpose at the cost of his soul which is betrayed into misadventure. It is to eliminate all such chances and possibilities of mishap that orthodox spiritual tradition frowns upon and strongly discourages occult lines of effort in which intercourse with the beings of other worlds is not rare. But we must remember at the same time that all the Devatas or deities are not of this type. There are benevolent deities who answer equally readily to the prayers of the devotee and their help is inestimable for him if only he keeps his Ideal pure and aloft. If he aspires only for the Highest the deity helps him, takes him a long way, not merely with spiritual aid but help of other kinds as well. The Tantra Shastra has done signal service in emphasising that though all the devatas are of the same divine origin, yet each has a special stress in its character, each is meant to actualise and help to actualise the particular potentiality of the Supreme in creation. Thus certain deities have it within their power to confer wealth, material and spiritual, some to confer health of mind and body, some have an exclusively spiritual function. It is again a fact to be noted that prayer to an indefinite something, to an Impersonal divinity can only evoke an impersonal or indefinite response. If a response is sought to be evoked for a particular need, the prayer could be fruitful when it is addressed to a canalised centre of the Divinity, the Personal form which is active for the purpose in question, and that is precisely what the Devata in its higher sense is in the Tantra. Spiritual progress with the help of deities as these is rendered easy and safe. The sincerity with which the seeker puts himself to their care guarantees safety against the rocks and steeps in the path, the progress is smoother and the growing realisation richer by reason of the happy contribution made and especial gifts conferred on him by these chosen deities, *Ishta-devatas*.

The Tantra Shastra develops the means wherewith to commune with the Gods is rendered possible. Man is endowed with faculties all of which are not active or perceptible to the physical mind, but are nonetheless real; and given the necessary touch of awakening and opportunity for development they function with much more effect and with an infinitely larger range than the usually active sense-organs. The ancients knew this and developed various lines of discipline for the development of this less-cared-for and hidden side of man in which lies the means for his deliverance from helpless subjection to the bonds of physical nature. There are many lines of Yoga, including Hatha Yoga, Mantra Yoga, Raja Yoga, Laya Yoga, not to speak of Devotion and Knowledge, each with its own basis, technique and process of functioning and the seeker has to choose in accordance with the aptitude of his nature and demands of his soul the proper way he would commence. Now the Tantriks took over these Yogas, as they were, improved upon them with their special knowledge of the occult worlds and applied these means for opening up the inner centres that window upon the supraphysical and still higher regions. But they did not stop with that alone. They developed another Sadhana whichalso had significant origins with the Vedic

Rishis—the *mantra.* The Mantra-sadhana has survived to this day as the most significant contribution of the Tantras to the spiritual heritage of mankind. A Mantra, as is well known, is not a mere letter or collection of letters, with some meaning. It is the sound-body of a Power charged with the intense vibrations of the spiritual personality of the creator or the seer of the Mantra. The Mantra is an ever-living embodiment of the Truth and Power which have found expression in it through the medium of the Rishi or Yogin who has given them that body. And when a Mantra is uttered, under proper conditions, it is not the feeble voice of the reciter that goes forth to evoke the response of the Gods to whom it is addressed, but the flame of *tapasya* and realisation, that is lying coiled up in the body of that utterance. The vibrations issuing from the Mantra are its own and they create the necessary conditions in and around the reciter appropriate to the reception of the response from the deity to whom the address is made. The form of the Mantra may be coherent words or may be single letters arranged in a certain order. The Tantra has thus formulated some seed-letters, *Bija-akshara*, which the seeker uses as the Mantra. These *Bijaksharas* have been endowed with a perennial store of power by the Tantric seers and it needs only the living touch of the Guru to set them awake in the disciple. This is the true sense in which the use of the Mantras is to be understood. They are not, as at times the superficial mind may be tempted to suppose, just convenient aids for concentration, mechanical devices for keeping the mind from wandering.

These are the essentials of the Tantra Sadhana—the Devata, the Mantra and the Guru. The Devatas are certainly not worshipped in the abstract. They are approached in the form in which they revealed themselves to the inner eye of these seers. For these Gods and Goddesses, though they may not have the physical form of the gross kind, have yet their own characteristic figure and colour. They have their own vehicles, *vāhana*, their auras of specific colour. Some of them reveal their presence in certain definite symbols.

All these are matters of experience with the Tantric seers who proceeded to render these subtle forms and figures in their physical correspondences as close and faithful as possible. Hence the sacredness and importance attached to the images and figures in the Tantric ritual. The image, *murti*, or the diagram, *yantra*, are the meeting places of the Invisible Presence of the Deity and the sense-bound soarings of human aspiration.

The Bijakshara, the Mantra of the seed-letter, is also no construction or invention of the imaginative Tantriks. These letters have an individuality of their own, their own shade and colour and reveal themselves as such. Each seed-letter refers to a certain principle related to the Tattwa of the Deity. And it could by itself be a Mantra or form a Mantra in conjunction with other seed-letters or words.

Then there is the Guru, who carries the Tantric tradition in himself, is instinct in some measure with the living presence of the deity invoked and who implants the Mantra along with the activating personal force of his own in the disciple. The

Mantra-dynamis is set in motion within the being of the disciple by the Guru and if only he would co-operate by assiduous attention and compliance with the needs of the growing Sadhana the progress is assured and the goal sure of reach. The Guru, the Deity, the Mantra are all equally important. The Shastra goes so far as to combine them in the identity of a single whole, and with reason. For the Guru is present in the Mantra through the influence he puts into it while initiating the disciple. The Devata is present in the Mantra which is indeed the Sound-body of the deity. Again the Devata is also present in the person of the Guru. And it is the Mantra which works out the Sadhana. That is why it is said, the Guru, the Devata and the Mantra are one, *guru-devata-manunām aikyam.*

Thus it will be seen that the Tantra Shastra attaches great importance to all the three essentials of the Sadhana. The Guru is much more than the physical appearance he wears; he is looked upon as the embodiment of the Deity sought to be realised or attained; to look upon him as a human being like any other is not merely wrong but also a dangerous delusion. Then there is the image in which the deity is worshipped. The image or the form is the 'material foundation' to form the 'physical nodus' for the act of external worship. To look upon such an image as mere stone is profane. Again the Mantra has a special character, it is the body of a spiritual truth or deity. To look upon it as mere letters is to blaspheme the sacred character of the Mantra. Thus the Tantriks have a famous dictum which sums up the Tantric position in regard to the Guru, the Image and the Mantra: "To hell he goes who mistakes the Guru for a human, who takes the image for a piece of stone, who looks upon the Mantra as mere letters."[1]

III

This, then, is the Tantric system in its fundamentals. We see that there is nothing

[1] देशिके मानवभ्रान्तिं प्रतिमासु शिलामतिम् ।
मन्त्रेष्वक्षरबुद्धिं च कुर्वाणो नरकं व्रजेत् ॥

in it which runs radically counter to the ancient spirit of the Vedic teachings. On the other hand there is much in conformity with it or in continuation of it. It has assimilated the Vedic spirit and revived it in a modified form. If there is a note critical and antagonistic to the Vedas in some of the extreme texts of the Tantra, it is in the nature of a rejoinder provoked by criticism of the later Vedists, the Smritikaras that the Tantra, unlike the Veda, has no sacred character about it because all castes, *varnas*, including women, have access to it, and such other insinuations. We have referred to the esteem in which they hold the Vedas. The central feature of the Vedic ritual, viz. the Yajna is taken up in the Ritual of the Tantra with suitable changes and there is no temple without a *Yāga-shālā*, Sacrificial Hall. The gods of the Veda continue to adorn the Tantric pantheon; their functions continue, but vary in form; the names undergo a change. The same gods are worshipped under different names and, what is remarkable, at times the very same Mantras and gods in the Rig Veda figure in the Tantra in all their grandeur. We shall illustrate this point as it is important to show how the Tantra has worked its way up to adumbrate in it the gods of the Vedic pantheon. We shall take an example from the Prapanchasara-tantra which deals with many deities, Vaishnava, Shaiva, Shakta without distinction of superiority of any one over the other.

Agni in the Rig Veda is a deity of paramount importance without whose help it is impossible for the sacrificer to proceed. Agni is the seer who finds the way, the *pāvaka* who burns the dross and cleanses the seeker of all sin and impurity, carries him through all obstacles, like a boat over the seas, *naveva sindhum*. In the Shakta Tantra the same Deity is worshipped as Durga, the indomitable, the protectrix who carries the devotee safe across the sea of misery, the ocean of birth and death, *bhavasāgara-nauḥ*. And what is more important, in one place the exact Mantra addressed to Agni in the Veda is applied here to Durga.

It is in the text referred to above that we

come across three Mantras which have been combined together to form a hundred letters and give what is known as the *Shatākshari Vidya*. The first Mantra consisting of 44 letters, in *trishtup* metre, is bodily taken from the 99th Sukta of the first Mandala in the Rig Veda.

Agni is the seer, knower of all. It lies in his power to render us all help as a result of his fore-knowledge. Knowledge is a most priceless possession of man and without it he is rudderless in the sea of life. And Agni deprives the enemy of this indispensable possession. To him, says the Rishi, let us offer our choicest gift, the very sap of life, the distilled juice of Ananda, the Soma, so that pleased, he would transport us over all the eddies and whirls, tides and waves of obstruction and misfortune that beset life. 'Like a boat across the waters,' is a favourite image of the ancients. It is repeated in the Upanishads, it also finds mention in the Tantric text referred to. Here is the Rik and the English rendering:

जातवेदसे सुनवाम सोममरातीयतो नि दहाति वेदः।
स नः पर्षदति दुर्गाणि विश्वा नावेव सिन्धुं दुरितात्यग्निः॥

'To the Knower of all Birth (Agni) we press Soma, to him who consumes the knowledge (or wealth) of the enemy. Let Agni carry us across all the obstructions like a boat over the river.'

In the Veda the Rik is ascribed to Rishi Kashyapa; in the Tantric text also the Seer of the Mantra is Kashyapa. There the deity is Agni, here it is Durga.

Then follows the second part of the Shatakshari (hundred-lettered Mantra) of 32 letters, in *anushtup* metre, which again is a verbatim reproduction of the 12th Rik in the 59th Sukta of the seventh Mandala in the Rig Veda. The Rik is addressed to Rudra as Tryambaka, father of the Three (worlds). The Rishi aspires towards immortality for himself and for others who have engaged themselves in the Yajna, the *antar-yajna*. He has a claim for immortality as a child of the Gods, a position he has attained not merely by his endeavours but by the benign grace of the Gods themselves. But this high status of immortality cannot be won and retained by any one without a certain elevation and strength of purity; the utmost that human effort can build up in the direction is inadequate. Only the Divine can promote and shape the requisite all-round strength and fitness. Again desire, want, greed, lust bring in their train disappointment, grief, unhappiness, disease and ultimately death. And for those that aspire for immortality there should be nothing in them which clings to its opposite, viz. death and agents of death. He that would share in the high status above has necessarily to be aloof and separate from, even while living amidst it, the envelope of ignorance and darkness that characterise the human world, like a cucumber separate from its shell, says the Rishi, like the ripe cocoanut loosened from its shell, say the saints and sages of later times.

त्र्यम्बकं यजामहे सुगन्धिं पुष्टिवर्धनम् ।
उर्वारुकमिव बन्धनान्मृत्योर्मुक्षीय मामृतात् ॥

'We adore the Father of the three worlds, Tryambaka of auspicious Fame, increaser of fullness and strength. May I be detached from Death like cucumber from the shell (or the stem,) not from the Immortal.'

In the Rig Veda, this Rik ascribed to Vasishtha is addressed to Rudra, as Tryambaka, father of the three worlds. Here in the Tantra also the deity is Rudra, as Mrityunjaya, conqueror of Death and the Mantra is famous as the Mrityunjaya Mantra.

The third part of 24 letters, in *gayatri* metre, is the famous Gayatri from the 62nd Sukta of Rishi Vishwamitra in the third Mandala of the Rig Veda. Savitr is the deity in the Veda; the same supreme deity is invoked here also. Savitr, it must be noted is identified with Vishnu here as in the Rig Veda. Vishwamitra is the seer of the Mantra here also. The Sun, Savitr, is not the physical sun we see in the skies, but the supreme Effulgence in the highest firmament above, beyond the lower triple creation. The physical sun is indeed taken as the image of the Truth-Sun, the Centre of all Knowledge and radiating Power. It is the radiance issuing from the

Supreme Source in which is massed all the creative movement of the Uncreate that is the ultimate root of all movements in the creation. Let that Light motivate and energise our thought-movements, says the Rishi.

तत्सवितुर्वरेण्यं भर्गो देवस्य धीमहि। धियो यो नः प्रचोदयात्॥

'We meditate upon that excellent splendour of the Lord Savitr. May he activate our thoughts.'

One significant fact shall not escape notice here in as much as it illustrates the remarkable facility with which these seers reconcile the claims of the respective votaries of Vishnu, Shiva and Para Shakti for supremacy. Thus here in this single Vidya, there is Durga who stands for the Para Shakti of the Shakta, there is Rudra in place of Shiva and there is Savitr, Surya for Vishnu. All are placed on the same supreme level of adoration, all are simultaneously invoked in the prayer poured forth by the Sadhaka.

Such is the synthesis of the Tantra, broad-based and deep-rooted, catholic and progressive. It does not ignore or overlook any past heritage of spiritual value. Its Jnana-pada, the metaphysical basis, combines in itself the essence of the Vedantic philosophy with all the spirit of pliability and catholicity of the ancient Rishis. The Yoga-pada, the practical side, revives the remnants of past lines of Yoga as far as possible and carries further the esoteric tradition, absorbs and develops the later physico-vital and psychological methods of self-development and self-exceeding. The Kriya-pada, the social and the ceremonial aspect, takes up the institution of community worship and ritual from immemorial times and extends the claim of the Spirit on the entire society. The Charya-pada, bearing upon personal conduct, re-establishes the claim of society on the individual and reconciles it with the special privileges and responsibilities of the latter issuing from his spiritual transcendence.

THOUGHTS ON TANTRA

WE propose to consider certain features of Tantra Shastra with special reference to Chandi, famous as Durga.

Upadhyaya is a Tantrika; he knows the art of propitiating the spirits—deities as he calls them—and averts certain sorts of evil that may otherwise befall his clients. Among other things, he knows and puts into practice with remarkable success a curious art. He casts a spell over a given area, definite and reasonably limited of course, and goes away, and that becomes a prohibited area for the cobra. This man's method has nothing to do with the tact of the snake-charmer or the use of any material means to rope in or drive out the venomous reptile. An incident which took place just a few weeks ago would go to point out the character of the genuine magic, or we may add, of the occult significance of the phenomenon we would presently relate.

We may call it superstition, but it is a popular belief, quite often verified and therefore dynamic that to kill a cobra is fraught with danger to the killer and to the household that is, or promises to become, its home or a resort of its frequent visitation. Now this happened in the sister's house of my young friend who returned here a fortnight ago after paying a short visit to his ancestral home. Thus, it is a first-hand report since he was present there at the time and mention of the details would repay the attention paid to it. The family with children has been living in the house for many years; but all on a sudden, one day a cobra was sighted within their lodging, to the annoyance of the inmates. Certainly there was awe, but awe with a dash of an almost religious sentiment. The hooded creature became a frequent visitor, unharmed, naturally unwanted. What was to be done? To their good luck, Upadhyaya in his itinerary had come to the township. When he was approached with the problem, he agreed to take up the question. He sat for a while and did some ritual, very simple and formal, got up and said "I have done the thing, *dig-bandha*; the quarters are closed, the fence is completed, the enclosure is impenetrable." Next day, what took place was indeed amazing. The cobra did not turn up, but that itself may be account ed for somehow, as due to causes other than the magic of the *māntrika*. But the miracle of a mongoose running about in the house in place of the cobra, solved the problem of the family, while winning laurels for the Upadhyaya.

We can give by all means our own explanation, that the man was in contact with the spirit *kshudra devata* presiding over the cobra group, or some other explanation. The Tantrik says he consulted his goddess, she consented to help him. Whatever way we look at such a phenomenon, it remains a fact and cannot be explained away. Well, this is undoubtedly a Tantric act.

Similar and still more remarkable incidents which are brought about by human agency through unusual powers are within our personal knowledge and enable us to conclude that those who wield such powers are usually ignorant and do not know how they get them, but know the occult formulae, the technique, or even have the influence and capacity transmitted to them by an adept in the field. But all these are generally despised by people whose lives are influenced by religious or moral sentiments. Yet these go by the name of Tantra. Usually, the Tantrik of this sort does not prosper even in the ways of ignorance, lives a miserable life, ends his life in misery.

Such practices in some form or other are not confined to this country. A journalist hailing from England toured this country some years ago and wrote a book in which he devoted sufficient number of pages to Spirituality in India and in illustration of it gave an account of his meeting a genuine famous saint. What he wrote was informative and proved useful to many who were drawn to the subject and to such centres of genuine spiritual Force to which he had made reference. The book made him famous overnight, we might say deservedly, so much that he came to be looked upon as a Guru himself by some good people. But later when he went to search for some genuine magic in Egypt, he saw and learnt many things about cobras and giant scorpions and wrote again; but it was a steep descent from the sublime to the ridiculous, a fine illustration of the contrast between spirituality and spiritualism.

There are certain Tantrik books which are indeed abominable; some of them are published and available in the market, but are definitely wicked. The misleading element lies in the titles of these books such as Siddha Shankara Tantra, Dattatreya Tantra etc. and quite often in the childish, if not mischievous sham that the subject-matter purports to be all instruction or information that Shiva once upon a time gave to Parvati. But we need not dilate upon this despicable side of Tantra which includes not only transaction with the elemental spirits and other powers of a low order, but also the degradation of high ideals, of true spirituality of the Shakta cult into the "left-hand worship" *vāmāchāra*, represented by the five "M"s. But before leaving this lowest aspect of Tantra which in some respects corresponds to the spiritualism or spiritism of the West, and includes in a way the aims of the modern attempts of Mesmerism, Hypnotism and certain sorts of groping occultism, we may remark that the method employed depends upon external devices, uses of certain "occult" drugs which are believed to attract the spirit-force or spirit-being as well as certain figures and diagrams and secret code-words.

The Tantra Shastra proper,—leaving aside the lower forms and the baser accretions—is strictly the science of the Mantras. If on one side, it is vulgar and discredited, as briefly noted above, on the other side it is exalted, combines in itself the highest form of Yoga and knowledge and devotion so much so that it might be termed a synthesis on broad lines of practical methods pursued by aspirants of different persuasions. By the use of the Mantra, mystic syllable or syllables, powers of concentration are developed to open the centres that are ordinarily closed in the human system. And these centres, when opened, become steps in the staircase, in the rising tier of Consciousness functioning as windows upon a wider and wider existence, of a larger world teeming with forces and beings whom one may contact on the way or ignore and move onward towards the highest reach, the Supreme Consciousness. The Tantric Yoga at its highest aims at realisation of the highest Consciousness and the powers natural to it. There are certain features that distinguish it from other Yogas of which brief mention here may not be out of place. Certain lines of Yoga can be practised without any serious belief in the existence of God, a higher Intelligence, and one can indeed meet with success if the aim be the usual control of mind, a certain mastery of vital functionings in the body and increase in the vital capacity for holding the will and exercise of the breath control and mind control, and concentration leading to trance. Certainly, Raja Yoga can be practised, not to talk of Hatha Yoga, without any devotion to or faith in God. Faith in the Guide, the Guru, faith in the efficacy of the line followed, faith in one's own capacity to achieve the end in view—this threefold faith is enough, but necessary, as indeed it is necessary for the Tantrik Yoga also, while in the latter the element of devotion with faith in the higher power and grace of Shakti is *sine qua non* from the very beginning. And it has an advantage over Jnana Yoga in that it relies and depends upon the guidance of the Shakti for the fruitful course of the discipline followed. We thus see that the Tantra aims very high, and the practice carries within it the essentials of many disciplines.

II

Now that we have briefly noted the two extreme sides of the Tantra Shastra, we shall proceed to consider here a question connected with Mantras that is generally ignored by scholars who deliberate, philosophise and write upon the subject. It is perfectly true that the aim of the Tantra is to achieve the Highest, and the Mantra is used as a means for concentration to open the centres of consciousness for the gradual unfoldment of knowledge and power leading to the ultimate goal. But we must pause here and see if the Mantra is just a mechanical device, means for concentration and nothing else. There is a truth often ignored by philosophers of Tantra, not by those who take to the Mantra

Sadhana. It is this that there are many deities with the Supreme Deity at the summit and through any of them, by his or her help, one can get at the Supreme or the Supreme can through any of the deities favour the initiate and give him the necessary lift. The point to be noted here is that the Supreme Deity does not negate or annul the existence of the deities but on the other hand uses them for her (or his) purpose or allows them free scope to deal with the Sadhaka in accordance with the spirit and manner of his approach. And these deities are realities, entities, beings with intelligence and power appropriate to the levels they occupy in the hierarchy of the grades of Cosmic existence. Once we recognise the fact that there are distinct Powers, beings whose influence man can receive, who can be contacted through proper means, we have accepted that the lower the levels they occupy, the easier the contact effected. It is this fact that accounts for the black magic part of the Tantra to which we referred as degrading and despicable. For there are good as well as evil forces and beings, spirits, evil especially on the levels that are nearer the Earth-plane.

But there are higher beings, with a larger field for their activity, with knowledge and power proper to their station and natural to the order they belong to in the Cosmic scale. There are still higher beings, Gods and Goddesses proper, with cosmic functionings and nearer to the Supreme Cosmic Godhead who presides over the creation. They are, one may say, vehicles, instruments, with distinct characteristics, and therefore individual Gods and Goddesses in that sense; they may be, some of them, in closer touch or conscious union with the Supreme Deity, whose work they carry out. Now the Mantra-sadhana claims to win the favour and grace of any of these, not necessarily for reaching the supreme goal, though there is always that possibility. The Sadhaka aims at first to be in the good graces of the God or Goddess, so that he can get the necessary guidance in life. As he progresses, and finds some measure of success in the Sadhana, if his deity happens to be a being of a lower order he may prosper for a time in the line of his choice, and very likely close his career in failure. If the deity of his choice be of a higher order and his Sadhana proceeds with certain signs of help from his *ishta devatā*, his progress brings about a change in his attitude to life, and his devotion to the deity grows stronger and stronger than his attractions to the aims of common life with which he may have started the Sadhana for success in life through the favour of a Devata. And in the end, the Sadhana naturally leads the Sadhaka beyond his first aims, either by fulfilling or cancelling them, to the larger and higher aim of life which indeed is the goal of all lines of approach to the Supreme. But if from the very start, the Sadhaka takes to the Mantra of any particular Personality and form of the Supreme Deity with the sole object of realising the highest through the favour of the God or Goddess he worships, and the Sadhana proceeds on proper lines, safe passage is assured and the burden of the Sadhana is taken on hand by the Deity in the long run, through various stages of communion and contact, and unmistakable touches of the influence or the Presence frequently sensed with certitude.

Mantra-sadhana proceeds on the basis that there are distinct Individualities, Gods, Goddesses with Forces and beings dependent on them and emanating from them, even as they themselves are emanations and personalities of the Supreme; and this fact will be evident from a casual perusal of source-books on Tantra-Shastra, and some of the standard books like Prapanchasara whose authorship is ascribed to Shankaracharya. But nowhere is it so pronounced and clearly brought to light as in the second and third section of the threefold Episode of the Devi-mahatmya to which we would refer later on. Here we shall confine ourselves to one question, the subject of Mantra itself. On the basis of the teachings of the Tantra Shastra itself, it is but proper to dismiss as puerile the apparently rational explanation of the use of the Mantra as a device for concentration. For in that case the Mantra becomes just one of the many mechanical devices that can be used,—a kith of crystal-gazing which also is a device. The Tantric claim is different, the Mantra is held to be a powerful instrument; itself is a power clothed in sound-symbol that is potent and lives in its sphere, and is meant to appeal directly to the deity for favour and help and ultimately to reveal the light and power and presence of the deity itself. The Mantra has an inherent power, but its manifestation depends upon the fulfilment of one of the two conditions: either the Guru who gives the Mantra must be a Mantra-siddha, an adept, capable of awakening the initiate to the deeper vibrations of the Mantra-consciousness; or the disciple must be ripe enough for awakening the Mantra-power to ring and pulsate with the inner consciousness or the deeper being in him that is the meeting ground for the worshipped deity and worshipping soul. If both the conditions are present, then it goes without saying that success naturally becomes easier. It is certainly true that what is achieved by the Mantra Sadhana can be achieved by other means also, by pure devotion or else by higher forms of Yoga for which all is possible, on principle. But that fact does not detract from the value and characteristic line of Mantra Sadhana, as a definite way of approach not only to a particular deity, but even to the Supreme. For it combines in itself devotion and concentration for a life disciplined to commune with the Devata which by itself can confer upon the Sadhaka all knowledge of Yoga and the opening of the inner centres of power and knowledge. This is possible of course when the Mantra-siddhi is accomplished bringing with it what is called *sākshātkāra*, the Presence and consciousness of it. Besides, in certain lines of Tantric Sadhana, the Mantra is looked upon as a sound-body of the Devata which fact is particularly stressed in the case of certain Mantras,—in this connection Shri Vidya is notable. Also, in the case of certain Devatas, prominence is not given to the repetition of the Mantra, but to the devotional aspect in which recitals play a dominant role, reinforcing the aspirational capacity enlightening the faith and will to achieve the end which is the attainment of the Anugraha of the adored Deity. Favour or even grace is not an adequate rendering of this Sanskrit word. For the expression denotes an act on the part of the Adored, an action with effect that continues without break, a gracious smile or glance that is cast upon the worshipper, who is seized and held in it so closely that time or place could not separate the human and the Divine, Jiva and Deva. This is the significance of the term, *anu-graha*, (*grah* to seize and hold, with *anu*, to pursue or follow i.e. without interruption.)

III

We have just mentioned the importance of recitals—what is called *Pārāyana*, in certain worship and this is specially applicable to the worship of Chaṇḍi as advocated in the Saptashati, the famous *Devi-māhātmya*. It is not that the Mantra-japa is not important or has no place in this cult. It has its place and importance for the purpose of *Japa*, inaudible repetition of the mystic syllables and *Dhyāna*, silent meditation. But the recital of the text assumes a greater importance in this worship because the text itself takes the place of the Mantra treated as sacred utterance of inspiration; it is surcharged with a purifying potency that clears the atmosphere and appeals in supplication, and with confidence for the manifestation of the presence of the Devi. A word is necessary here to draw the line of distinction between the Mantra for Japa and Mantra for recital. In the former, inward repetition in silence leading to concentration is the characteristic way, and the Mantra is usually short. It can be even a single syllable, what is called Seed-letter, *bijākshara*, and is related to a particular God or Goddess; it has its special feature, even subtle form and colour perceptible to the subtle vision, and in it is centred the gravity of the God or Goddess. Naturally, in such Sadhanas, the Yogic element with personal responsibility preponderates until the gracious Presence becomes clear, *prasanna*, and the Sadhaka receives the grace, *prasāda*, of the Devata. It is said of Ramakrishna Paramahamsa, that when he uttered a mantra, or a seed-sound, say Rum, Agni signified by the sound-symbol appeared to his vision with his occult native colour. But Paramahamsa was an exceptional case, because he was already in the Mother-consciousness and from there he could objectify any subtle truth, that is not manifest in the outer existence.

But the Mantra used in *pārāyana* is audibly recited, it has an effect on the surroundings, in the general atmosphere; it contributes greatly to the development of the devotional element which indeed becomes very effective as it progresses and invokes the Presence to dominate the place of worship and govern and guide the devotee. We may remark in passing that all devotional compositions, verse or prose or musical texts are not Mantras, nor are Mantras always in verse or in prose form. We must note the fact that the Tantric Mantra is usually short, even a single syllable packed with the force or the symbolic sense related to the particular deity. Occasionally, verses from some inspired poems or scriptural texts like the Saptashati are treated and used as Mantra. But the Vedic hymns are of a different order, they are all Mantras where the meaning is as important as the text, and generally meant for recitals, though a short verse may be selected for Japa and meditation on the meaning of the Mantra with devotion to the Devata, as is done in the case of the famous Gayatri. But usually all Vedic Mantras are used for recitals while a few selected passages have become famous as texts for Japa.

To return to the Saptashati. This is famous as a sacred text which occupies a special place as a Tantric scripture. There is no other work in the whole of the Tantra Shastra which enjoys such a deserved reputation as an assured and effective means for the worship of the Devi. It is a special line of approach to the Supreme Goddess Durga, 'not easy of access' to mortals as is meant by the term. Though Mahakali, Mahalakshmi, Mahasaraswati are her special Manifestations as spoken of in the text, they are not the same as those that come under the category of what is called the Ten Grand Sciences (occult and spiritual), Dasha-Mahavidyas. For the latter are different and independent, and each one of them is directly the Supreme Goddess communed with and worshipped in accordance with certain rules and rituals formulated in the respective Tantras. Here in this worship of Durga otherwise called Chandi, recital of the text is much more important than the Japa of the Mantra, not to speak of the rituals, though these have certainly their place in all Tantric worship as they provide for a material basis to form a nodus for the physical and outward act of adoration. So much importance is attached to the sacredness of the text that every verse in it is treated as a Mantra in the Katyayani Tantra. And this is done in spite of the fact that all the 700 verses do not describe the glory of the Goddess, as there are many verses which are narratives related to the origin and end of the stories of the Devi. Besides, there has been a tradition that the Chandi worship has a Vedic basis. How far and in what sense it is correct to say that this Durga worship has Vedic basis is a question we shall consider within the brief space we have set for ourselves here. But before doing so it is necessary to have an idea of the subject matter of the Saptashati. It is not necessary here to dwell at length on the details of the story as it is so popular and well-known and could be gathered from the simple and easy, though powerful, text itself or otherwise from translations. Let us then recall the whole story and state it in a few passages.

Two unlucky men meet in a forest, come to know of each other's pitiable plight, for one had lost his kingdom, and another all his wealth. They consult a sage there, who answers their questions, clears their doubts and at their request gives them instructions in regard to the worship of Durga. They carry out the instructions, engage themselves in worship and austere meditation, *tapas*, and at the end of three years, they had bestowed upon them, the Grace of the Devi who revealed Herself to them and granted their request. Suratha, the Kshatriya, got back his kingdom, while Samadhi, the Vaishya got what he asked for, supreme Knowledge. This is the story. Now, apart from instructions in the secrets of worship (*rahasyokta-vidhanena*) that the sage Medhas gave the two devotees at the close of their meeting, he first spoke to them of the Glory of the supreme Goddess, illustrating it in three episodes, *charitas*, of the Devi—the first related to Mahakali, the terrible Ruler of the Night, the Yoga-nidra of Hari, who is the destroyer of Madhu and Kaitabha; the second to Mahalakshmi, who makes an end of Mahishasura, and the third to Mahasaraswati, who deals the death-blow to Shumbha and Nishumbha. It is not possible to enter into a discussion of the significance of these exploits of the Goddess; for they must form part of a separate subject for consideration. Suffice it to note these events are not happenings on the Earth-plane, or of this age which is the cycle of Vaivasvata Manu. But the description of the battles between the Goddess with her Vibhutis and emanations on one side and the Asuras and their forces on the other are significant and throw light on happenings and activities in a different world and plane which have their bearing on Earth-life and human existence. Another notable fact is that there are truths hidden from our vision, regarding good and evil forces, *daivic* and *āsuric*, contending for supremacy over this world, this Earth whose fate quite often hangs in the balance, but is ultimately decided in her favour by the intervention of the Supreme Power, Mahashakti of the Lord of the Universe. And this will be evident to any casual reader of the Saptashati; there are memorable passages that often ring in our ears in which the promise of intervention in crises made by the Devi constitutes a scripture-monument to the Divine vigilance over human affairs on Earth. The inspiring verses in which the words of assurance are couched are untranslatable; yet even a feeble echo of it in English may convey something of the spirit breathed in these prophetic utterances that the sage-author of the Saptashati communicates to us.

In the first Charita we find the sage affirming "Though She is eternal, immanent in the whole Universe which is Her embodiment, She takes birth again and again, incarnates Herself in a special form of Her choice for the successful regime of the Gods, Devas—for establishing Divine Principles in the world-order that its functionings may increasingly harmonise with the eternal verities and higher laws of the creative Godhead." Again in the second Charita when the Gods regained their lost kingdom by the destruction of the Asura by the Devi and adored and sung her glory, the Goddess in Her grandeur, highly pleased, promises to come to the rescue of the Gods whenever there was need and they were put to trouble by the Asuric forces, the Demons. Similarly, in the third and the last Charita, when the task of the Mother was over, the Gods adored Her and chanted hymns in praise of Her prowess, of Her manifestations and of Her motherly heart, She was pleased and again gave Her word of assurance to stand by the side of the Gods in times of need and stress, and also declared that She would ever be present in places where, these hymns were recited and used in prayers. Finally the Devi speaks of Her future incarnations.

It is certainly a fact of religious experience of devotees even today that in such recitals and places of worship something of Her Presence, of Her Grace is felt and it cannot be understood, much less appreciated by those who have no inkling into or not cared to investigate into these aspects of life devoted to higher and godward life. Nor can these stories of Gods and Asuras and their battles be intelligible to those who seriously think that the Physical universe and material existence are the sole and fundamental Reality. Here we cannot resist the temptation of quoting Sri Aurobindo. The best way of understanding the meaning of these stories of battles between Gods and Asuras is to ponder over and grasp the sense and spirit of certain passages in his writings in a different connection. We shall quote a passage or two that will be helpful to the thoughtful reader to know for himself the import of such episodes.

"The soul of man is a world full of beings, a kingdom in which armies clash to help or hinder a supreme conquest, a house where the gods are our guests and which the demons strive to possess." "The soul is a battlefield full of helpers and hunters, friends and enemies, all this lives, teems, is personal, is conscious, is active."

A word more before we proceed to the question of the Vedic basis of the Chandi. This scripture is included in the Markandeya Purana. The Purana purports to be a dialogue between Markandeya and Kroshtuki. Therefore he is the sage, the Rishi, the seer, of the whole scripture. The mystical reverence in which the Devi-Mahatmya is held can be best understood if we remember a tradition that comes down to us through orthodox Vaidiks who are worshippers of Chandi. The Saptashati, they hold, is a great *Artha Shastra* i.e. a Shastra that teaches us the means of realising all ends in life, not *artha* in the restricted sense of wealth or Economics. Thus the standard texts for the four purposes of life, *purushartha*, are in order: Manu for Dharma Shastra (which is said to have been originally 700 verses), Devi-Mahatmya for Artha, Vatsayana for Kama (which also is said to have been at first 700 sutras) and the Bhagavad Gita for Moksha (which is also 700). Whether there is significance in the number 700 or not is not quite material for our consideration here. But the tradition shows that the aim of Saptashati is not in a limited or one-sided direction. It includes the aims of life here and the supreme purpose as well. And this is borne out in the story of Suratha and Samadhi by the Power and Knowledge they were respectively favoured with, for Kingdom represents supreme Power and enjoyment, *bhoga,* in the world. It is not an exclusive this-worldliness or other-worldliness whose fulfilment is vouchsafed in the Saptashati. Even when Suratha longs for regaining his lost kingdom, it is not the same old self of the miserable man that grabs at the power bestowed on him by the grace of the Goddess. For, before he started the Sadhana in accordance with the instructions he received from the sage, he understood and assimilated the truths about the Devi and the world and the cause of suffering therein, and thus qualified himself for a rigorous life and turned towards the Divine Mother; for only thus is an effective discipline possible, to earn and reçeive her favour and help. And it is necessary to note that the sage laid stress in the very beginning on the fact that all misery owes its origin to *mamata,* the sense of mine. Suratha, then, had the added difficulty of having the world-enjoyment by renouncing it as 'not mine,' *bhoga* by *tyaga*, while the man for Knowledge, Samadhi, the Vaishya, had unburdened himself of worldly cares and joys as well. Both started the same Sadhana, driven by misery; both changed, each in his own way. A few lines (free rendering in English) from the first chapter in which the sage expounds the root cause of all suffering and the remedy thereof would go to show the high aim of the worship advocated in the Saptashati.

"All creatures have a consciousness of their own and are instinct with the desire to preserve themselves and their knowledge is spread over the objects of senses. Of the created beings, some are born day-blind, some night-blind, while others are, day and night, of equal vision. The knowledge of man is in no way better than that of birds and beasts which show great skill in preserving *themselves* and what is *theirs*. Here again the sense and feeling of 'mine' is spread over all creation—man and beast alike; know then, the cause of all this is Ignorance, Avidya, which is not the creation of any being on earth or in heaven. It is a product of the workings of Mahamaya, the great illusory Power of Lord Vishnu. She is the power for bondage as well as for liberation, for ignorance and for knowledge. By Her the whole universe is set in motion revolving incessantly and containing in it all that is mobile and immobile. She, in short, is the Power of Hari, the Lord of the Universe—called Yoga Nidra, the Sleep-power of Yoga or the super-conscious poise of the Supreme Being."

Now we will turn to the Vedic basis of the 'Chandi'. It is traced to the 125th hymn of the tenth Book of the Rig Veda. We get the clue from a line in the closing verses of the Saptashati where it is stated that the Devi Sukta was being used for Japa "*devisuktam param japan*". But we do not find anything in the Rig Veda relating to the story, ritual, or forms of worship mentioned in the Saptashati. But if we look into the spirit and substance of the Vedic hymn, we do find for the first time, also for the last time in the Rig Veda, thought and spirit and Mantra-force vying with one another in revealing and making felt the

Divine afflatus in the Riks of Vak, Ambhrini. For the latter name is patronymic, she the seer, Rishika, being the daughter of Ambhrina. Her name itself is Vak. She sees the revealed truths of the Godhead, finds the inspired word to give expression to them in the shape of this hymn of eight verses. There are many hymns in the tenth Book of the Rig Veda where we find that the name of the seer, Rishi, is also the name of the Devata. This can be explained by the fact that in such hymns the seer is one with the Devata, experiences and lives in conscious union with what he adores; and it is such realisations that account for the identity of names as in the hymns of Vaikuntha, Lava and others. But this is not to say that there are not to be found such realisations recorded in the other Mandalas of the Rig Veda. But there quite often the Rishi's name is addressed in such a way or with a double meaning that it is applicable to the God spoken of in the Rik. There are other seers who speak of their realisations of the supreme Being on the dynamic side and proclaim "I am Manu, I am Surya...."

as is to be found in the hymns of Vamadeva in the fourth Mandala. But there the seer's name is retained separately.

Here, in the case of the Devi Sukta, though the seer's realisation of identity with the Supreme Vak, the Creative Word, which in the language of the Tantra is Para Shakti, may account for the identity of the Name, (Vak as applied to the Rishika as well as to the Devata) it will be more correct to say that the Female Energy of the Supreme Godhead, *para-devata*, realising Herself in or choosing the embodiment of Vak Ambhrini, utters the Word, the Mantra. This is at once in consonance with the proclamation made in the Vedic Hymn, and the spirit and substance of Saptashati. Let us then close the subject with an English rendering of the famous Hymn[1] —the Devi Sukta, leaving the reader to ponder over the mighty words of 'Vak' and see if it is not in line with the high thought, spirit and purpose of the Durga Saptashati.

[1] RV. X. 125

अहं रुद्रेभिर्वसुभिश्चराम्यहमादित्यैरुत विश्वदेवैः ।
अहं मित्रावरुणोभा बिभर्म्यहमिन्द्राग्नी अहमश्विनोभा ॥१॥

1. I walk with the Vasus and Rudras, with the Adityas, as also with the All-gods, Vishva Devah.

Mitra and Varuna, both I hold aloft, even so Indra and Agni I do, and the Ashwin-twins too.

अहं सोममाहनसं बिभर्म्यहं त्वष्टारमुत पूषणं भगम् ।
अहं दधामि द्रविणं हविष्मते सुप्राव्ये ३ यजमानाय सुन्वते ॥२॥

2. I uphold and cherish the Soma that is to be pressed out (for the delight of the Gods) and am the supporter of the Divine sculptor Twashtri, and of Bhaga and Pushan. I hold the wealth for the sacrificer who reaches to the Gods the pleasing offerings of Soma and Havis.

अहं राष्ट्री संगमनी वसूनां चिकितुषी प्रथमा यज्ञियानाम् ।
तां मा देवा व्यदधुः पुरुत्रा भूरिस्थात्रां भूर्यावेशयन्तीम् ॥३॥

3. The Queen, I am the dispenser of wealth; conscious, I am the first among the Gods (for whom the sacrifice is meant).

Such am I (the One) and the Gods have found me established in the Many, permeating and taking possession of the Manifold (existence).

मया सो अन्नमत्ति यो विपश्यति यः प्राणिति य ईं शृणोत्युक्तम् ।
अमन्तवो मां त उप क्षियन्ति श्रुधि श्रुत श्रद्धिवं ते वदामि ॥४॥

4. It is by Me (by the sole Power) that one eats his food, sees, breathes and hears what is said.

They that ignore me (with their thought not turned to me) run to ruin. Hear, I declare to thee, the truth of faith, hearken!

अहमेव स्वयमिदं वदामि जुष्टं देवेभिरुत मानुषेभिः ।
यं कामये तं तमुग्रं कृणोमि तं ब्रह्माणं तमृषिं तं सुमेधाम् ॥५॥

5. Of my own accord, I announce this (truth) which the Gods as well as men strive to reach.

Whomsoever I love, I make him mighty, him a Brahman, him a Rishi, him a man of pure understanding.

अहं रुद्राय धनुरा तनोमि ब्रह्मद्विषे शरवे हन्तवा उ ।
अहं जनाय समदं कृणोम्यहं द्यावापृथिवी आ विवेश ॥६॥

6. For Rudra I stretch the bow—for the destruction of the tyrant, of the Veda-hater (Brahma-dvit). On the people I bestow equal joy in battle and I have permeated Heaven and Earth.

अहं सुवे पितरमस्य मूर्धन्मम योनिरप्स्वन्तः समुद्रे ।
ततो वि तिष्ठे भुवनानु विश्वोतामूं द्यां वर्ष्मणोप स्पृशामि ॥७॥

7. I gave birth to the Father (Heaven) at the summit of This (creation, Earth), My origin is in the Waters in the Inner Ocean.[1] Thence I extend pervading all the worlds; and yonder Heaven I closely touch and penetrate with the showering and flowing body of mine, *varshmana*.

अहमेव वात इव प्र वाम्यारभमाणा भुवनानि विश्वा ।
परो दिवा पर एना पृथिव्यैतावती महिना सं बभूव ॥८॥

[1] Ocean is the image of the Infinite Consciousness and Being—in the conception of the ancients; the word 'inner' before the 'ocean' (antas-samudra) here removes the veil over the Truth indicated by Ocean and Waters, *samudra* and *apah*.

8. Like the winds I blow vehemently, myself commencing all the worlds; far beyond the heavens, far (beneath) the Earth—so vast by my largeness I have become.

PRATISHTHĀ (INSTALLATION)

(In the Light of His Wisdom)

SALUTATION to Sri Aurobindo, to the Master who has just left the body, but has kept here the light he ensouled in incessant radiation for the fulfilment of his proclaimed mission.

We need not consider here the question of the grand Idea, the sublime Truth, he embodied; nor need we dwell on his achievement in the realm of the Spirit and its sequence that intimately concerns us, or its bearings on the aspiring soul of man in general. That is a subject that directly relates to the core of the Master's Personality which we keep aside for the present. But there are certain luminous sides of his central grandeur which have found their expressions in the colossal edifice of his *literary* products. They shed the same light of wisdom everywhere in the diverse branches of knowledge handled by him. Whatever the subject, Art or Poetry, Philosophy or Religion, Politics or Social Science, we find the same light illumining the contents, the same wisdom elevating us to take a fuller view of the horizons of the concerned realm of the subject and thus enrich ourselves in the mind's dimensions or regions of the soul. It is in the light of this wisdom that we propose to study one aspect of the Tantric path which is an important element, the soul-principle, so to say, of image-worship. We leave aside for the present the synthetic character of the Tantric Yoga and inner worship to which attention hasbeen drawn earlier. Here we confine ourselves to a single limb of the Tantric worship and make an attempt at elucidating the underlying principles on which the whole structure of ceremonial worship is based. Here we must bear in mind the value and necessity that the Tantrics have discovered for the dedication of the whole man to the Godhead, the Mother of the Universe, with the material body for the pedestal. The significance of the body as the temple is quite often stressed, so much in detail that every part is considered to be the abode of particular Gods and Goddesses, the aides of the Supreme, the higher Powers in the Cosmos, while the central spot is the lodgement of the Supreme. Hence an all-round purification of the body as the sacred temple is emphasised and many devices are resorted to, including at times material means for keeping the physique intact and fit for arduous discipline, *tapasya*, by which alone one can have control over the forces that are adverse to the progress and success of the Sadhana. Hence also, the Tantra deems it essential to inculcate the doctrine that no worship of the Deity is complete without the worship of the Deity's body in a material image—an idol or a picture or some symbol in the physical world.

Here it may be stated that the outer symbol of worship is considered an indispensable object of adoration by the Tantric devotee to whom it is not a mere symbol. The image, the idol is a consecrated object, vivid in a subtle manner, is charged with the presence or power of the Deity whose Grace is invoked, and this is so especially when properly installed by an adept, or with the help of an expert guide, *Acharya*. A fuller expression of devotion involves the worship of the body of the Deity as well as the maintenance of purity and holiness in the body of the worshipper. This is the position of the Tantrik in regard to the external aspect of worship.

An incident may be cited here in this context, which will be of much interest to the seeker and devotee who may discover his own explanation of the matter, as explanations are always conditioned by one's culture and temperament, general disposition and equipment for understanding things that are supernormal. It is now more than forty years. A young man in his early twenties witnessed an unusual way of worship conducted in the house of an elderly Tantric devotee. The latter was a friend of the youth's father; so, with due respect he had earlier spoken to him of his doubts about the validity of such worship, *bāhya puja*. The gentleman was a strictly orthodox Vaidik Brahmin, a Sanskrit scholar specialised in Nyaya, a Pundit employed in a Government College and so had a secure means of supporting his small family and keeping it above wants. He had ample leisure as the hours of his teaching work in the college were few. He devoted the rest of his time for religious purposes, with special devotion to the Right-Hand worship, *dakshina achara* of the Tantric way. He was no magician of a low sort. This much has to be said in order to enable the reader to get into the spirit of the man's daily performance of worship.

When the youth had finished what he had to say about the *mantrajapa*, the Pundit looked at him for a while and then said, 'You say that you have done this mantra and that, and have observed the rules according to the Shastra and even though you were properly initiated while quite young and did repeat many lakhs of these mantras, you have not found the results as stated in the books. Well, I am sufficiently old, you are my old intimate friend's son; I take the liberty of speaking to you about certain things in my life, for that may be of some use to you. I too, when young, was like you initiated in *Sri Vidya* by my father, and have continued it to this day, and would continue even to the end of my life whether or not I see the result as spoken of in the Shastras. Such has been my faith all along. But something happened a few years ago which gave a definite turn to my line of Sadhana and worship.' Here he paused and then spoke with feeling: "One day I was reciting verses in praise of the Great Goddess and felt intensely, saying to myself, 'O Mother, I have been Thy worshipper all these years, I know no other God than Thee, Thou hast not vouchsafed to me Thy favour, Thou dost not reveal Thy presence to me in any way.' This feeling lasted for some time and though the intensity slowly thinned, the attitude was there. But nothing happened in response to my cry. A few days later, one night I had a dream. I could not retain it when I got up; but there was a feeling that it was a curious dream in which some one said, 'You will see what happens in two or three days. Accept it, worship it.' There was something more and clear but I could not recollect it. I did not pay to this interesting occurence as much attention as it deserved. But, two or three days later, quite unexpectedly when one evening a man appeared before me and spoke a few words, the whole dream came to my vision in a trice. He placed a *danda* (a rod) covered with a cloth, and said 'Now, I go. You will do as directed; all your difficulties vanish from now on.'

"Now it was eventide; I thought I might begin the Puja then itself. Since then I have been doing it, quietly. If you want, you can stay a little longer. I am coming." So saying, he went in and took his bath, and was preparing to start the worship that day. Before the commencement he said: "When the Puja is over, I will be silent for some time. You can receive the *prasad* and go home. And if you want you can come any other day. You may be struck with wonder and may have to think about what you are going to witness at the Puja time. I tell you beforehand one thing; the *danda* is the divine weapon of Subrahmanya, Kumara, Son of Devi; its worship is the worship of its wielder, i.e. Skanda. It is the command of the Devi whom

I worshipped all my life that I should worship her child and achieve the fulfilment of my life. I have a reasoning mind, I am a *tarkika*, logician, I know that learned people in their wisdom ridicule outer worship as a thing meant for the beginners or fools. It is not for others' good opinion, praise or applause that God has given us life. Inner worship is certainly essential, it leads more to Yoga and Jnana. Outer worship intensifies devotion and is powerful and effective and supplements one's Sadhana. At present I care more for outer worship, I see the presence of Kumara in the Danda. You too will see now. More about this some other time. It is getting late. I shall start. Remember what I have spoken to you. Do not look down upon external worship. It is effective, when there is the proper Installation, *pratishthā*. God bless you." Instantly the Puja began, there were one or two people, assisting him to burn incense and bring the necessary vessels of which a glittering brass or bronze plate is the most important, for in the centre of that plate he was to place the object of his worship with small idols, representing gods and goddesses, *parivaras* who surround their chief, Kumara, the *pradhana devata*. In a low voice uttering *mantras* he took the Danda and muttered a *mantra* somewhat inaudibly; he was motionless, holding his breath for a while. The observing youth could make out that it was the *mantra* usually used for installation, *prana-pratishthā*. The Danda, the rod, was a little less than three feet in height, about half to three-fourths of an inch in diameter at the bottom and more or less the same throughout except at the top where it was a little more thick and circular with a knob at the head on which was engraved some figure. He held the *danda* in a perpendicular position with both his hands in the middle, or a little above the middle. He held it in silence with eyes closed for a few minutes and muttered something removing his hands. As he did it, the Danda, to the amazement of the new-comer, instead of falling, without any support, began to swing pendulum-wise with the knob quite often coming almost half-way to the ground. Slowly the swinging stopped, and the Danda stood erect, quite steady and fixed of its own accord. The Puja began, with the sacramental bath, *abhisheka,* to the deity, the *danda,* and with other usual ceremonial details. When the worship was over the youth received the *prasad* in silence and left the house as previously advised by the Shastri.

The youth thought: "Is there any mechanical device which makes the stick stand in the middle of the plate erect without support? Everything was done in my presence. The Shastri is a sincere man, quite genuine in his speech and action. Can it be after all that there is something in the *pratishthā mantra* which is the means of instilling some force into the inanimate thing? But I have done the same *mantra* many times before and have experienced nothing of the kind. But the man had earlier spoken of certain preliminaries as requisite to realise the efficacy of these *mantras*". Thus a hundred and one thoughts crossed his mind on his way home. But somehow he did not meet the Tantrik again for he was led to owe allegiance to other worthies until in his middle age an obliging

Destiny led him finally to take refuge at the feet of Sri Aurobindo.

To return to the subject of outer worship: even for the external worship in the Tantric system, a certain inner purity is considered necessary. Where this is not possible, some one who has it and has achieved and seen some tangible results enabling him to guide the worship, has to do the *pratishthā* of the Image or *Yantra*, the symbolic mystic Diagram in which the presence of the Devata is invoked to be vivid and felt by the worshipper. Once it is done, it is to be tended in a devotional atmosphere which grows in intensity in the course of time. And this is applicable not only to the personal worship of an individual, but also to centres of public worship, such as temples and other *pīthas*, seats of spiritual power.

Here it must be noted that there is a distinction to be drawn between the *pratishthā* of a *mūrti*, an image, or a *Yantra* for the personal worship of an individual and that for the public worship in a temple. In the former instance according to the Tantra Shastra, a novice is guided by a genuine priest for external worship but the *upāsaka*, the worshipper himself must prepare in course of time to call down the presence of the deity; for this purpose he has to undergo preliminary disciplines into which many elements enter; of these what is called *bhūta-shuddhi* is the most important and even indispensable both for the outer worship as well as for the *mantra-sadhana* which leads to the inner life. The literal meaning of the term is the "purification of the elements"; but its effect is to cleanse the atmosphere in and around the person of the worshipper and clear it of the influences of the elemental forces or beings, the lower spirits, the blind unintelligent forces to which men in their ordinary lives are subject; and the weaknesses on the mental or moral plane that pertain to the material body of man are indeed the result of the play of these forces of universal nature. The loosening and ultimate riddance of the Tamasic forces of the dense and elemental nature is indeed *sine qua non* for qualifying oneself for the *mantra sadhana* that aims high at contacting the deity in the deeper layers of one's consciousness or on the higher levels of one's being that are supra-physical. But it is also necessary and to some extent possible in the case of a beginner preparing for the external worship, *bāhya-pujā*. For without the *bhūta-shuddhi*, the *prāna pratishthā* could not be done, since the latter is meant to evoke the presence or power of the deity from the spirit of one's own being which itself is lodged in, and a portion of the supreme Self *parama ātman*, the indwelling Godhead in all creatures. In fact, the Tantric works everywhere reiterate the value and necessity of this purification without which the *pratishthā*, the installing of the power and the presence either within oneself in the inner worship, or instilling the spirit and power into the image or symbol in the outer worship is not possible. The outer worship, as is done commonly by the generality of devotees, will be ineffective without the essential *pratishthā* on which everything else depends.

We shall return to the subject of *pratishthā* after we have done with one or two points in regard to the *bhūta-suddhi*. Its basic importance in the *mantra sadhana* cannot be too much emphasised, since in the yogic path of the Tantrik it affords the foundation on which the whole edifice of Yoga is raised, with devotion, knowledge and will as its constituent elements. But even before entering straight into the inner apartments of Yoga where the psycho-physical centres are concentrated upon and opened for progress in the Sadhana and building the inner life, the Tantrik beginner devoted to his chosen deity is advised to effect the *bhūta-shuddhi* without which the presence of the deity cannot be felt, and the grace of the deity, even when it comes in response to an ardent call of the *upāsaka*, worshipper, or a fervent emotional appeal to the deity, could not be properly received or even when received be adequately held and effectively retained in the vessel, the body. Hence its importance and its value are recognised for any form of serious worship. It must be noted here, that the purification of the various limbs, outer physical and the inner mind-stuff aims not only at the eradication of the narrowing and obscuring influences of the elemental forces and the universal weakness of the lower Nature, but inviting in their place the opposite good influences of the benign forces, the powers of the supra-physical worlds. That is why in the actual *bhūta shuddhi* every part is offered to a deity, and the group of deities that are invoked to occupy their places in the body-vessel, *ādhāra*, constitutes indeed the minor gods who are the *parivāras* of the chosen Chief, *pradhāna*. In some Tantric works, instead of the minor gods and the chief Deity, the *tattwas* or cosmic principles with the soul, and the Supreme Self for the Chief Deity are mentioned in the culmination of the *bhūta-shuddhi*. And this is to give a pure spiritual turn with a philosophic basis to the *upāsana*. As the space set for this short study precludes the citation of such texts which are numerous and well-known, at least one well-known authority like the *Meru Tantra* may be mentioned here in this context. Here is an English rendering:

"When the body in its entirety becomes fit

to commune with the Devata, one must restore and fix in their proper place the principles, *tattwas*, hidden in the self. (For this purpose) from the heart-lotus one must bring out the soul from the supreme self. And according to the rule (method) by means of the Hamsa Mantra one has to look upon the body as a luminous form of light and as having become quite competent for the worship of the Deity."[1]

This is just an instance out of many to show that the conception of the Tantrik in regard to the body was so complete and ideal that all the *tattwas* (or the higher powers) are understood to be lodged in it and the supreme Godhead abides in the centre and depths of one's being, the heart-lotus. Nor is the purification of the body and preparing it for Divine

[1] संजाते सकले देहे देवतोपासनक्षमे।
आत्मलीनानि तत्वानि स्वस्थानि प्रापयेत्ततः॥
आत्मानं हृदयाम्भोजादानयेत् परमात्मनः।
हंसमन्त्रेण विधिवत् तेजोरूपम् कलेवरम्॥
देवतोपासने योग्यमुत्पन्नमिति भावयेत्।

worship achieved by sheer physical purity and strength to be decided by medical opinion and judged according to hygienic standards. For the purity of the kind in the body is to be accomplished in such a manner that the god or gods could discover in it their actual temple consecrated for their advent or manifestation. And indeed the body is the field of battle between the dark and the luminous forces in the Cosmos, engendering bad will and good will with their brood of feelings and ideas and their consequent subtle effect on the body, nerves and muscles, in the shape of ill-health and good health and general dis-harmony running riot in the system. Thus the *bhūta shuddhi* has a double function, the negative and the positive, the former paving the way by the clearance of the disagreeable forces for the positive side, i.e., the filling of the purified parts by the presence of the Powers that are invoked to occupy their right places in the system.

While this *shuddhi* is the real factor that effectuates the *mantra-sadhana* and the principle underlying the inner worship of any deity, not to speak of the yogic way leading to the opening of the centres, *chakras*, it is necessary also for *bāhya pujā* to be effective. A word about the chief means employed for this fundamental purification by the Tantrik must be stated here.

Apart from a certain refinement in the course of one's conduct in life involving the elevation of mental and moral sides which are generally held incumbent on the initiate, the main instrumentation is as a matter of course, the *mantra*, the sound-symbol of the deity. It is a sound-expression of the idea that at once veils to the gross sight and reveals to the inner eye of vision the body of the deity, of the truth to be realised. And this truth, the Devata, dwells in the subtler worlds, in the higher planes, not on the physical level, in the world of the senses. Hence the repetition of the sacred word, the *mantra*, prepares the being to be collected, composed, and concentrated on the single will to achieve the object of the worship, the Grace of the Deity, to feel and perceive and commune with the Presence. But a mere mechanical repetition runs in a futile circle. For the *mantra* to be potent, the guide's help, i.e., the Guru's initiating capacity counts much. For he awakens the latent faculties in the disciple. This is the secret of the *mantra sadhana*. The Tantric scriptures discourse upon the qualifications of a disciple and the qualities of a competent Guru on which we need not dilate here. Sri Aurobindo expounds the rationale of the *mantra-japa* in the light of yogic psychology and experience to which attention may be drawn here: "The word is a sound-expression of the idea. In the supra-physical plane when an idea has to be realised, one can by repeating the word-expression of it, produce vibrations which prepare the mind for the realisation of the idea. That is the principle of the *mantras* and of *Japa*. One repeats the name of the Divine and the vibrations created in the consciousness prepare the realisation of the Divine."

We have stated this much about the *mantra* as a means for effecting the purification of the elements as a preliminary, most important for the *sadhana* and inner worship in the Tantric path, and generally recommended for the outer worship also, though here the worshipper has to rely entirely upon an unshakable faith reinforcing his devotion. As has been already stated, the material object of worship is often an image or occasionally the *Yantra*, for instance, the famous *Sri Chakra* or similar symbols of the dwelling place of the Deity. Here, generally, the presence of the Deity is evoked on behalf of the ordinary worshipper, by an adept, an expert in the field. But this practice has in course of time degenerated into a sort of priestcraft—an unlearned and crude *purohit* muttering the mantras without meaning them, i.e., without caring for a knowledge of the *mantra*, not to speak of the spirit which he is supposed to instill into the image to be worshipped. This is called *prāna-pratishthā*, the infusing of life and soul into the sacred symbol. Here *prāna* really connotes, as in the earlier Upanishads, a conscious-force emanating from the supreme Soul in which the individual being abides. It is an obvious fact that this can be done effectively only by one who is equipped for the task by a successful course of training in the performance of purifying his own being as described earlier. It is only such an adept, a true Acharya who can do the *prāna-pratishthā* of the Image for worship on behalf of another individual. The Tantrik attaches importance to worship because he recognises that devotion to God cannot be complete without laying one's body in full offering at the service of the Deity whose presence is evoked and installed in the image. The famous nine limbs[1] of devotion of the Vaishnava are applicable to devotees of other cults also and the Tantric path being in essence synthetic in character incorporates into it among other things, the elements of knowledge and devotion, and discovers the value of bodily service to the Deity. And in the words of the Master, if the external worship is done 'with the true consciousness, it can bring the greatest possible completeness to the adoration by allowing the

[1] Hearing of the name of God, singing his glory, constant remembrance, worship of His feet, worship with flowers, adoration, servility friendship, and last self-offering.

श्रवणं कीर्तनं विष्णोः स्मरणं पादसेवनम्। अर्चनं वन्दनं दास्यं सख्यं आत्मनिवेदनम् ॥

body and the most external consciousness to share in the spirit and act of worship.'

So far about the personal image-worship by an individual devotee the efficacy of which is certainly conditioned by his faith and devotion. Here we may proceed to consider the question of *prāna-pratishthā* of the image meant for public worship such as that in temples, and also the subtle and occult principles underlying the traditional belief in worship at what is generally believed to be holy places, not necessarily or invariably temples where images are installed. In this connection we may recall to our mind what Sri Aurobindo states in his usual assured tone in mentioning the *prāna-pratishthā*, the essentials of which he puts in a nutshell in the following passage in a letter to a disciple. Let us quote the letter[1] as it is of inestimable value for our purpose:

"What you say is no doubt true, but it is better not to take away the support that may still be there for the faith of those who need

[1] Published in the *Letters*, Second Series, p. 239.

such supports. These visions and images and ceremonies are meant for that. It is a spiritual principle not to take away any faith or support of faith, unless the persons who have it are able to replace it by something larger and more complete.

If the *Prāna-pratishthā* brings down a powerful Presence, that may remain there long after the one who has brought it has left his body. Usually it is maintained by the bhakti of the officiant and the sincerity of belief and worship of those who come to the temple for adoration. If these fail, there is likely to be a withdrawal of the Presence."

The Image installed is just a support for the external worship, for the satisfaction of and a steadying influence upon the outer mind and being; the real and substantial element is in the Presence or Power so installed by a great soul. But a Siddha, one who has achieved substantial results in the spiritual path need not install an image for the benefit of others. The very spot he lives or lived in becomes charged with an emanation of the presence and power of his holy soul so much so that anyone susceptible to subtle or occult influences can feel and detect the abidance of something non-physical in the physical surroundings of such a place. This accounts for the holiness of places where great sages and seers have lived, stationed in their Tapas-Force, or have shed their mortal frame and mortality.

There is another important aspect of this question of worship at, and pilgrimage to, holy places which may be mentioned here for the benefit of minds that are inclined to believe that any famous place or temple held to be holy and attracting crowds of people from afar and near need not necessarily be holy or exert benign influence or elevate the spiritual side of man. For it is perfectly true that when a presence or power is brought down where the image is installed, it remains a live force for a long time and continues even after the man passes away. Tradition, indeed, nourishes the faith of the people who visit such places for worship. But there are certain temples and other places of worship without an image installed where the Power, the presence is not brought down by any holy man and without any tradition to that effect. Still, such places attract large crowds of persons many of whom are convinced by experience of the active presence of a superior Force granting boons to many a worshipper. Here the truth of the matter is that such places are chosen and occupied by beings of a supra-physical world —let us call them beings of the vital world— who exercise their influences from those centres which afford a physical support for contact with the earth and earthy beings. These beings are quite often spirits of a low order whose workings are more easily and palpably felt and certainly in the end injurious to a healthy mind and a soul that has taken to the spiritual way of life. This accounts for the centres of worship which draw numerous people over whom the spirits have a sufficient sway for their own gratification and enjoyment.[1] But

[1] My first preceptor Vasishtha Muni it was who acquainted me with these occult truths among others, and years long after when I came here I found the Mother's utterances and authentic knowledge of these matters of detail in the occult realm confirmed them.

there are good, not only evil beings of the vital world and they too exercise their benign influence over men who come to worship; but such temples or places are less numerous. Thus it will be seen that all temples need not have Images of worship installed by a holy man. There are many which are the self-chosen places of spirits and other beings of the vital world; they bring themselves, and need not be brought down by any one, to places that afford them sufficient support through the desires and passions and other hungers of men which are enough to feed such deities. When the support is withdrawn and men turn to higher forms of worship, they vanish to their native country of the vital world, or roam about in search of a suitable habitat on earth made possible through the prayers rich with greed and other weaknesses of the inviting human beings on earth who are ignorant of of what they are doing.

Another point must be noted in regard to the matter of holy places. There are certainly holy spots the origin of which could not be traced with any certainty. But it is intelligible on the basis that in the very formation of this globe, there are certain spots which are conducive for meditation and concentration and they engender a spiritual atmosphere which can be sensed and felt by those who are by nature or training sensitive to subtle and occult influences. It is also on this basis that the Tantra Shastra quite often recommends, for its votaries a mountain-top or the bank of a holy river etc., *parvatagre naditire*, for *mantra-sadhana* in solitude.

Such is the value of a holy atmosphere for purposes of spiritual life. But nothing is holier than the name of the Guru, for it carries laden with it the influence and power and the very presence of the Guru, if he is a competent Guru, one of real stature in the realm of the Spirit, say, a perfected soul, a *siddha*, a great Vibhuti of high spiritual force. For in such cases the Guru has done the installation, *pranā-pratishthā*, of his very presence in the heart of his disciple whose fidelity to his master is enough to nourish it for its growth and fruition in the receptacle that is the devotee, the *sishya*. If the name of the Guru as stated above is holy for the disciple, what is holy beyond measure for all spiritual aspirants and devotees is the spot where such a *siddha* or *vibhuti* or—and this is rare—a Divine Manifestation lives, or lived in *tapasya*, and shed the coils of mortality—the 'material envelope.'